Gil G. Noam
Editor-in-Chief

NEW DIRECTIONS FOR YOUTH DEVELOPMENT

Theory
Practice
Research

spring | 2005

Participation in Youth Programs

Enrollment, Attendance, and Engagement

D1611605

Heather B. Weiss
Priscilla M. D. Little
Suzanne M. Bouffard

issue
editors

JOSSEY-BASS
A Wiley Imprint
www.josseybass.com

PARTICIPATION IN YOUTH PROGRAMS: ENROLLMENT, ATTENDANCE, AND ENGAGEMENT
Heather B. Weiss, Priscilla M. D. Little, Suzanne M. Bouffard (eds.)
New Directions for Youth Development, No. 105, Spring 2005
Gil G. Noam, Editor-in-Chief

Microfilm copies of issues and articles are available in 16mm and 35mm, as well as microfiche in 105mm, through University Microfilms Inc., 300 North Zeeb Road, Ann Arbor, Michigan 48106-1346.

NEW DIRECTIONS FOR YOUTH DEVELOPMENT (ISSN 1533-8916, electronic ISSN 1537-5781) is part of The Jossey-Bass Psychology Series and is published quarterly by Wiley Subscription Services, Inc., A Wiley company, at Jossey-Bass, 989 Market Street, San Francisco, California 94103-1741. POSTMASTER: Send address changes to New Directions for Youth Development, Jossey-Bass, 989 Market Street, San Francisco, California 94103-1741.

SUBSCRIPTIONS cost $80.00 for individuals and $170.00 for institutions, agencies, and libraries. Prices subject to change. Refer to the order form at the back of this issue.

EDITORIAL CORRESPONDENCE should be sent to the Editor-in-Chief, Dr. Gil G. Noam, Harvard Graduate School of Education, Larsen Hall 601, Appian Way, Cambridge, MA 02138 or McLean Hospital, 115 Mill Street, Belmont, MA 02478.

Cover photograph © Digital Vision.

www.josseybass.com

Contents

   Participation in out-of-school-time programs confers many benefits for
   young people, but many youth do not participate in programs. Understanding participation as a three-part construct of enrollment, attendance, and
   engagement can help stakeholders to maximize participation in and benefits
   from programs.

   Research from the perspectives of youth can illuminate reasons that they do
   or do not enroll in out-of-school-time programs. This information can help
   increase program participation, particularly for ethnic minority youth, who
   are traditionally underserved in programs.

   Youth and family characteristics predict which youth are most likely to
   participate in organized out-of-school-time activities and how likely they
   are to benefit.

   Out-of-school-time programs can increase youth participation using a set
   of promising strategies and a school and community-wide commitment to
   implement them.

Editor-in-Chief's Notes

The Significance of Enrollment, Attendance, and Engagement

ONE OF THE GREATEST challenges in youth programming is that hopes and expectations are typically not aligned with facts and reality. We want young people to join out-of-school-time activities to decrease their social isolation and risky behavior and to increase their passion in learning and school achievement. But youth often do not want to come daily or even regularly, and thus it becomes impossible to have sufficient "dosage" to accomplish these ambitious effects. Even if youth love the program sufficiently and make a strong commitment, it is not clear that the high expectation placed on programs can be met. Consider how many hours youth spend in schools, yet the results are so often mixed. A prerequisite to reaching any goal a program aspires to is that young people, especially those at an age where they can decide for themselves how to spend time after school, will attend.

Moreover, the fact that young people can choose to join or to stay home forces youth workers to deal with their consumers the way schools never have to. It leads to a view of young people as partners in the educational process, providing choices that build on their talents. We can study the process of learning and engagement far better under conditions of choice than in situations of mandatory presence, as in schools, where most of the learning research takes place. When and why do young people show up at programs, and when do they stay away? It is very important for our field to shed light on this "showing-up phenomenon." It is the foundation

NEW DIRECTIONS FOR YOUTH DEVELOPMENT, NO. 105, SPRING 2005 © WILEY PERIODICALS, INC.

for any outcome and an indicator (though not a proof) that something is happening.

I wanted this often-overlooked area of program development and evidence-based youth work to be addressed in *New Directions in Youth Development*. For that reason, I solicited an issue from Stanford University researchers Ben Kirshner, Jennifer O'Donoghue, and Milbrey McLaughlin on the topic of youth participation (issue 96). It was primarily focused on activities and programs that empower adolescents to participate and engage. I was lucky to have a great team of colleagues at Harvard to whom I could turn to address research and practice on participation in a new way. Heather Weiss, Priscilla Little, and Suzanne Bouffard were interested in focusing on this topic based on their research on enrollment, attendance, and engagement in out-of-school time. It makes a great deal of sense to focus on these three elements that organize the everyday language of programs: How do programs get youth to show up? What can they do to retain participants and join in regularly? And once they are there, how can they ensure they will be engaged by participating in meaningful activities?

Although it is important from a research point of view to separate the constructs into independent variables, they are not separate at all. If activities and relationships are meaningful, youth tend to come and become attached to programs and people. If youth can get engaged with friends, they want to attend. And conversely, it is impossible for them to be engaged if they do not attend with some regularity. Despite this interconnection, it is essential to study what the connections really are, how strong they are, what young people define as engaging, and what level of regularity different subgroups strive for. The issue editors have assembled an excellent group of researchers to make productive contributions to the interplay of these elements and have extended the question to include information about gender, culture, and race. We still know far too little about the significant issues that face every program that works with youth.

What is important to recognize when dealing with the questions posed in this issue is that after-school youth settings are different from most other social institutions, like the schools, family, or peer group. I have introduced the concept of intermediary space in previous issues of this journal to depict the nature of this particular social space: it belongs to no one, it needs to be managed collaboratively, and it is based more on participatory planning and service delivery than on bureaucratically handed-down directives. That might change over time, as one or another force might gain some hegemony. But funding patterns and coordination needs make it more likely that different players with different constituencies and goals will jointly shape the field of time after school.

The field has moved into prominence by at least three movements that have begun to move closer: prevention, youth development, and school reform. Each of these is making a special contribution to the intermediary space of good after-school programming. I believe that understanding how to engage youth so they come to programs regularly is tied to how to achieve the goals of these three movements. For example, prevention and public safety advocates want young people to attend regularly to protect youth and to protect society. Programs that cannot retain youngsters are deemed as not performing their duty. Those interested in school reform want students to be in programs regularly to gain additional time on task through homework and an academic focus. However, they tend to weigh the regularity in after-school programs against the need of students to be active in the school when school is out: around sports activities, theater productions, and clubs. Youth development staff tend to have yet another set of priorities. Although they want young people to come to their programs regularly, they typically believe that programming has to be based on what youth want and that this ability to choose also has to include the choice of joining. Boys and Girls Clubs and YMCA, for example, have been careful not to force young people to come against their will or for amounts of time where they have to choose to be "in or out." Thus, the expectations for attendance and engagement are quite different. It also makes for problems when these movements collaborate to create policies, expectations, and practices for this intermediary space yet are not truly aligned. As always, it is the youth who will point out these contradictions or act on them in their choices. This *New Directions* issue takes us to the next step in this important exploration and discussion and will not be the last one dedicated to this topic.

Gil G. Noam

Editors' Notes

A KEY ISSUE for all stakeholders working to improve non–school hour experiences for young people centers on youth participation in out-of-school-time (OST) programs. Practitioners want to know how to attract and sustain participation as a key step in maximizing their efforts to improve outcomes for youth. OST funders are invested in understanding how to measure participation in meaningful ways. With scarce resources, policymakers want to know how much participation is enough to improve youth outcomes. Addressing these needs for knowledge is especially salient for efforts to attract and serve young people who are at risk for social and academic problems. Although these youth are often targeted by community programs and are the ones who can reap the largest benefits from participating in OST programs, they are the least likely to participate. There is evidence to suggest that once youth are engaged in OST programs of sufficient quality for an ample amount of time, they experience measurable positive effects. Yet there is little information, especially for youth at risk, about the factors that contribute to getting youth in the door and keeping them engaged, a critical missing link in our understanding of participation and its links to outcomes.

Recognizing that we were at a rare juncture where the worlds of policy, practice, and research all agree that understanding participation matters is critical and that shared dialogue is necessary to bring us to the next level of understanding with the end goal of improving practice, the Harvard Family Research Project (HFRP) at the Harvard Graduate School of Education hosted a one-day meeting to discuss participation in OST programs—what it means, how to measure it, and how to improve it. With support

NEW DIRECTIONS FOR YOUTH DEVELOPMENT, NO. 105, SPRING 2005 © WILEY PERIODICALS, INC.

and leadership from the C. S. Mott Foundation, as well as the Nellie Mae Education Foundation and the Wallace Foundation, forty leading researchers, evaluators, practitioners, and funders in OST participated in a day-long conversation, peppered with panel presentations that unpacked key components of what HFRP now calls the participation equation: participation = enrollment + attendance + engagement. This issue of *New Directions for Youth Development* presents and expands on the information from that meeting and as such provides collective food for thought to practitioners, researchers and evaluators, policymakers, and funders, all working to improve the lives of young people through regular, meaningful attendance in the diverse set of OST programs operating throughout the United States. Throughout this issue, the term *out-of-school time* is used to refer to a range of non–school hour activities and programs that are offered to youth ages five to eighteen. This includes after-school programs, extracurricular activities offered by schools, community-based programs, informal leisure pursuits (such as reading and talking on the telephone), private lessons, mentoring, and tutoring. Taking into account this range of activities, the issue provides research-based strategies on how to increase participation and how to define, measure, and study it, drawing from the latest developmental research and evaluation literature.

Chapter One, by Heather Weiss, Priscilla Little, and Suzanne Bouffard, presents the conceptual framing of our model of participation that places the participation equation as central to achieving positive outcomes for youth. We point to the important role that contextual predictors play in determining participation, as well as issues of access and program quality. Integral to this framing chapter is a review of the potential benefits of program participation and some of the previously identified barriers to participation. The chapters that follow help unpack the three components of the participation equation: enrollment, attendance, and engagement. Starting with the first part of the equation—enrollment—in Chapter Two, Lynne Borden, Daniel Perkins, Francisco Villarruel, and Margaret Stone use the voices of youth to examine the question,

"Do I wish to participate in this program?" from a youth perspective, providing data from their work on studying participation among ethnic minority youth. Next, Sandra Simpkins, Marika Ripke, Aletha Huston, and Jacquelynne Eccles provide an in-depth look in Chapter Three at two key predictors of participation enrollment, gender and socioeconomic status, using data from two samples of low- and middle-income youth and their families. Chapter Four, by Sherri Lauver and Priscilla Little, provides research-derived strategies to attract and sustain youth participation, highlighting key features of program quality, as well as promising program practices, that are effective in getting youth in the door. In Chapter Five, the issue moves to the topic of measuring attendance. Leila Fiester teams up with colleagues at HFRP, Sandra Simpkins and Suzanne Bouffard, to outline the numerous reasons for collecting attendance data, as well as the importance of taking a more nuanced approach to doing so. Finally, Chapters Six and Seven examine engagement as it relates to participation. In Chapter Six, Todd Bartko provides the ABCs of sustained engagement, adapting a model developed to understand school engagement. In Chapter Seven, Deborah Vandell, David Shernoff, Kim Pierce, Daniel Bolt, Kimberly Dadisman, and Bradford Brown conclude this issue by describing new research that attempts to tease out the difference in activity, emotion, and engagement between OST program participants and nonparticipants.

In soliciting chapters for this issue, we intentionally requested that the authors make explicit the ways in which their research can inform program practice, and so they provide recommendations on such topics as how to accurately measure attendance; how to successfully recruit youth into programs, especially in the light of research on cultural differences in participation; and how to meaningfully engage youth in programs so that participation is more than just "being there."

We thank the entire HFRP Out-of-School Time Team for their support and contributions to this issue of *New Directions for Youth Development*. Their continued dedication to the Out-of-School Time Evaluation Database and our other core work is invaluable.

We also thank the C. S. Mott Foundation, which has supported our OST work since 1999 and provides invaluable scaffolding and leadership for all of us working to improve the lives of young people through the implementation of high-quality OST programs.

Heather B. Weiss
Priscilla M. D. Little
Suzanne M. Bouffard
Editors

HEATHER B. WEISS *is the founder and director of the Harvard Family Research Project at the Harvard Graduate School of Education.*

PRISCILLA M. D. LITTLE *is the associate director of the Harvard Family Research Project and the project manager of HFRP's Out-of-School Time Learning and Development Project.*

SUZANNE M. BOUFFARD *is a research analyst at the Harvard Family Research Project and a doctoral candidate in developmental psychology at Duke University in Durham, North Carolina.*

Executive Summary

Chapter One: More than just being there: Balancing the participation equation

Heather B. Weiss, Priscilla M. D. Little, Suzanne M. Bouffard

The research and evaluation evidence is mounting: out-of-school-time (OST) programs can keep young people safe, support working families, and improve academic achievement and social development. Over 6 million children are enrolled in after-school programs nationwide, but an estimated 14.3 million children still care for themselves in the nonschool hours. Because of this discrepancy, OST stakeholders need information about how to maximize participation in OST programs. The Harvard Family Research Project (HRFP) has developed a conceptual model, based on scholarly theory, empirical research, and knowledge gained from providers, that describes the characteristics that predict participation in OST programs as well as the potential benefits of that participation. In the center of the model, participation is conceived as a three-part construct of enrollment, attendance, and engagement. This equation serves as the basis for framing this issue of *New Directions for Youth Development*.

The chapter provides an overview of why participation in OST programs matters for young people, describes some of the barriers and challenges to youth participation, teases out more precise definitions of participation, and presents HFRP's conceptual model of participation. It focuses on the participation equation and concludes

NEW DIRECTIONS FOR YOUTH DEVELOPMENT, NO. 105, SPRING 2005 © WILEY PERIODICALS, INC.

by highlighting some overarching themes that recur throughout the issue and that have an impact on future directions for research and evaluation.

Chapter Two: To participate or not to participate: That is the question

Lynne M. Borden, Daniel F. Perkins, Francisco A. Villarruel, Margaret R. Stone

Do I wish to participate or not to participate in this program? That is the question that young people ask themselves when considering a new opportunity. What can be done to increase the likelihood that they will choose to participate in out-of-school-time (OST) programs?

This chapter describes a qualitative study that examined reasons for participating or not participating in OST programs. Some common reasons emerged, but the study also revealed differences among youth from different ethnic groups. It is clear that those who design and conduct programs must understand the processes through which diverse adolescents initiate their participation in programs and either persist or drop out. Given the apparent benefits of active participation in youth programs, it is important to remove barriers and increase access and, equally important, design programs that are of interest to youth in the contexts in which they live.

Chapter Three: Predicting participation and outcomes in out-of-school activities: Similarities and differences across social ecologies

Sandra D. Simpkins, Marika Ripke, Aletha C. Huston, Jacquelynne S. Eccles

The majority of research on out-of-school-time activity participation has focused on its relation to academic and social development, presumed to be consequences of participation, rather than on antecedents or predictors of participation. Understanding who participates in these programs can assist program directors in improving and sustaining youth involvement.

This chapter uses data from two research study samples to examine differences in children's activity participation based on family social ecology and child gender and how the relations between participation and outcomes vary based on sample, gender, and activity type. Although children in both samples were of roughly the same age and were assessed for similar outcomes, their family incomes, socioeconomic status, ethnicity, and neighborhoods were very different. Findings suggest that participation in activities varies depending on the young person's social ecology, age, and gender. Furthermore, participation in activities was typically associated with positive youth outcomes, but these relations varied depending on the level of youth participation, type of activity, and social ecology.

Chapter Four: Recruitment and retention strategies for out-of-school-time programs

Sherri C. Lauver, Priscilla M. D. Little

Many out-of-school-time (OST) practitioners seek ways to maximize enrollment, enhance frequency of participation, and ensure retention in OST programs, so that the multiple potential benefits of these programs are realized. Three critical areas of program quality are important underpinnings for success in recruitment and retention of youth in OST programs: a sense of safety and community; committed program staff; and challenging, age-appropriate, and fun activities. In addition, a review of over sixty OST evaluations reveals five promising recruitment strategies to boost enrollment: (1) matching the program to participants' needs (offering activities not readily available elsewhere or offering flexible schedules), (2) demonstrating the importance of participation to young people and their families, (3) reaching out directly to youth and their families in their homes and communities, (4) recruiting in peer circles, and (5) making a special effort to recruit at-risk youth. Finally, the evaluation literature points to five promising strategies to enhance regular participation and long-term program retention: (1) sending a clear message that regular attendance is important; (2) setting realistic goals to promote regular attendance, especially as youth grow older; (3) finding a balance among academic and other activities; (4) using incentives; and (5) keeping teens involved with opportunities for leadership, community service, and paid employment.

Chapter Five: Present and accounted for: Measuring attendance in out-of-school-time programs

Leila M. Fiester, Sandra D. Simpkins, Suzanne M. Bouffard

Evidence is emerging that youth who attend out-of-school-time (OST) programs more frequently and for longer periods of time benefit more than youth who attend less frequently or do not attend at all. It is also increasingly clear that children and youth will not reap the benefits of programs if they do not attend regularly. Collecting attendance data can help program leaders gauge demand for services, plan and manage programs effectively, and evaluate participant outcomes in relation to attendance.

This chapter presents these and other reasons for collecting attendance data, as well as the methods and techniques that program leaders and researchers have at their disposal for measuring attendance. It describes four indicators of attendance—absolute attendance, intensity, duration, and breadth—that can provide detailed information and insight about youth participants and their use of programs. The chapter also provides tips for collecting attendance data and features examples from OST programs. Throughout, the chapter illustrates that the right indicators and data collection methods depend on program needs, characteristics, and goals.

Chapter Six: The ABCs of engagement in out-of-school-time programs

W. Todd Bartko

The rapid growth of out-of-school time programs over the past five years has resulted in a dramatic increase in opportunities for young people. However, many programs have been ill defined, without appropriate attention to the developmental needs of children and adolescents and without the necessary elements in place to fully capture the interests and talents of youth.

In this chapter, the author shows how constructs drawn from research in education can be applied to research and practice in the out-of-school-time arena, in an effort to learn how the field can more fully engage young people in activities and programs. With more and more research indicating positive connections between participation in safe, supportive, and challenging activity settings and healthy psychological and social adjustment, attempts to encourage engagement rather than casual participation are warranted. Researchers and practitioners need to be mindful that engagement results not just from showing up, but from the interplay of the affective, behavioral, and cognitive experiences of youth in these settings. Suggestions for designing growth-enhancing contexts that increase the likelihood of engagement are offered, as are suggestions for future research in this area.

Chapter Seven: Activities, engagement, and emotion in after-school programs (and elsewhere)

Deborah Lowe Vandell, David J. Shernoff, Kim M. Pierce, Daniel M. Bolt, Kimberly Dadisman, B. Bradford Brown

Experiences that are deeply engaging and enjoyable, engender full concentration, and present a balance between challenge and skill promote children's development. This chapter describes a study that sought to identify the kinds of settings and activities that foster engagement and, by extension, positive youth development. The after-school experiences of 191 ethnically diverse youth living in three states, some of whom participated in after-school programs and some of whom did not, were studied. Youth were equipped with logbooks and watches that were programmed to signal at random times. When signaled, youth recorded their location, social partners, activity, and feelings. The study found pervasive differences in the experiences at programs and elsewhere. Youth spent more time in academic and arts enrichment, organized sports and physical activities, community service, and homework at programs versus elsewhere, and they spent less time eating and watching TV at programs. They also reported higher levels of motivation, engagement, and positive affect at programs. At the same time, there were few differences in activities, emotions, effort, or motivation of program participants and nonparticipants when both groups were elsewhere. The similarities in these experiences while elsewhere suggest that the program context, not differences in youth characteristics or interests, was responsible for the feelings of engagement that were reported at programs.

Understanding participation as a three-part construct of enrollment, attendance, and engagement can help stakeholders maximize participation in and benefits from out-of-school-time programs.

1

More than just being there: Balancing the participation equation

Heather B. Weiss, Priscilla M. D. Little, Suzanne M. Bouffard

THE RESEARCH AND EVALUATION EVIDENCE is mounting: out-of-school-time (OST) programs can keep young people safe, support working families, and improve academic achievement and the civic and social development of young people.[1] Indeed, according to recent polling data, 6.5 million children are enrolled in after-school programs nationwide and therefore are poised to reap the benefits of program participation.[2] However, an estimated 14.3 million children still care for themselves in the nonschool hours,[3] thus not experiencing the unique opportunities that OST programs provide for learning, development, and safety. Furthermore, there are discrepancies in access to programs that impede equitable participation across youth of diverse backgrounds. Public Agenda reports that program participation differs between low- and higher-income children, as well as between minority and nonminority children. Low-income and minority parents are considerably less likely to report that it is easy to find programs that are affordable, run by

NEW DIRECTIONS FOR YOUTH DEVELOPMENT, NO. 105, SPRING 2005 © WILEY PERIODICALS, INC.

trustworthy adults, conveniently located, high quality, and/or interesting to their children.[4]

This discrepancy compels stakeholders working to improve non–school hour experiences for young people ages five to eighteen to seek information about how young people can better use their nonschool hours by participating in OST programs. Practitioners want to know how to attract and sustain participation to maximize the potential benefits to those participating, as well as how to reach historically hard-to-reach youth and their families. OST funders want to know how to measure participation in more meaningful ways in order to tease out the impact of their investments. With scarce resources, policymakers want to know how much participation is enough to improve youth outcomes. These issues are especially salient for youth who are at risk for social and academic problems. Although these youth are often targeted by community programs and are the ones who can reap the largest benefits from participating in OST activities,[5] they are the least likely to participate.[6] There is evidence to suggest that once youth are engaged in OST activities of sufficient quality for an ample amount of time, they experience measurable positive effects.[7] Yet there is little information, especially for youth at risk, about the factors that contribute to getting youth in the door and keeping them engaged, a critical missing link in our understanding of participation and its links to positive outcomes.

Based on previous research, the Harvard Family Research Project (HFRP) has developed a conceptual model that describes participation in OST programs and activities. In our model, scholarly theory, empirical research, knowledge gained from practitioners, and existing theories of change about how OST participation influences outcomes converge to describe influences on youth participation in OST programs and activities and potential outcomes of that participation. In the center of the model, participation is conceived as a three-part construct of enrollment, attendance, and engagement. This equation serves as the basis for framing this issue of *New Directions for Youth Development*.

Participation matters

When youth participate in high-quality school- or community-based OST programs, they are likely to benefit in a myriad of ways: they receive personal attention from caring adults, explore new interests, receive academic support, develop a sense of belonging to a group, develop new friendships with their peers, take on challenging leadership roles, and build a sense of self-esteem independent of their academic talent.[8] Youth's constructive use of their out-of-school time is a protective factor that has been associated with (1) academic achievement (higher grades and grade point average), recovery from low academic performance, and an interest in furthering their education; (2) a stronger self-image; (3) positive social development; (4) reductions in risk-taking behavior; and (5) better school behavior and fewer absences.[9] In fact, evidence increasingly shows that youth participation in quality OST programs influences current outcomes, which have an impact on outcomes into adulthood.[10]

Attendance in OST programs is predictive of academic success as measured through test scores, absenteeism, school dropout rates, homework completion, school grades, and course enrollment.[11] Research also shows that attendance is related to more prosocial and less aggressive behavior with peers, multiple aspects of friendships, and lower feelings of depression and problem or delinquent behavior.[12] Finally, some suggest that OST programs can provide the opportunity to develop critical "twenty-first-century" skills that include problem solving and interpersonal and communication skills, as well as proficiency in the basics.[13]

This information is based on a binary concept of participation: Did youth participate or not? But there is some evidence to suggest that children who attend OST programs more frequently demonstrate greater benefits from them as a result.[14] Higher levels of attendance in OST programs have been significantly correlated with scholastic achievement, higher school attendance, more time spent on homework and positive extracurricular activities, enjoyment and effort in school, and better teacher reports of student behavior.[15]

Challenges and barriers to participation

The potential benefits of OST programs cannot be achieved if youth do not attend. Unfortunately, low attendance is the norm in many OST programs for middle and high school youth. Indeed, a recent review of four large after-school evaluations clearly demonstrates that attendance in after-school programs is sporadic and short-lived across the elementary through high school years.[16]

For example, the evaluation of the national 21st Century Community Learning Centers (21st CCLC) program revealed that average attendance was 1.9 days a week for elementary students and 0.9 days a week for middle school students.[17] Assuming that a typical program operates about 2.5 hours each afternoon, this means that the average participating middle school student in the 21st CCLC program received only 32 days, or about 80 additional hours of enriching activity during the school year.[18] Similar low attendance rates have been reported at other programs. At the San Francisco Beacons Initiative, youth attended, on average, between 1 and 2 days a week.[19] The weekly attendance of participants in the various programs involved in the Extended-Service Schools Initiative averaged between 1.2 and 2.4 days, depending on the age of the child.[20] Similar low levels of attendance have been observed in several other programs, including the After School Education and Safety Program (formerly the After School Learning and Safe Neighborhoods Partnerships Program) and the Maryland After School Community Grant Program.[21]

Many factors contribute to low OST attendance, including a participant's desire to relax and "hang out" with friends; the very real need to work and generate family income; family responsibilities such as caring for younger siblings; boredom or disinterest; and safety and transportation issues. Furthermore, it appears that attendance dwindles during the critical transition from elementary to middle school, when youth continue to need caring adult role models and interesting out-of-school activities but do not need the direct and ongoing supervision necessary for younger children.[22]

But even if these barriers can be overcome and youth attend programs more frequently, the nature and quality of the time they spend in the program is critical to the desired outcomes. Larson has shown that youth can experience a combination of high motivation and cognitive concentration in organized OST activities.[23] In contrast, youth experience low motivation with high concentration during school and high motivation with low concentration when hanging out with friends. The unique combination of high motivation and high concentration in OST activities provides an opportunity for children to develop a sense of initiative. In fact, Hansen, Larson, and Dworkin found that youth reported not only experiencing more initiative but also more learning experiences (including interpersonal and personal learning, such as leadership) in extracurricular activities than in school or while hanging out with peers.[24] Theoretical and empirical work by Eccles and colleagues suggests that OST activities may also provide a context for youth to explore and define their identities.[25] However, a key ingredient to observing these outcomes is the ability of the programs to attract and sustain meaningful engagement over time for all young people.

What is participation?

Many researchers and evaluators use the terms *participation* and *attendance* interchangeably to refer to the amount of time young people spend in OST programs. Indeed, in their review of twenty-seven research and evaluation studies that examined youth outcomes in relation to participation, Simpkins, Little, and Weiss found that all of the studies used these terms synonymously to report outcomes associated with program attendance.[26] However, in her guide to measuring attendance in after-school programs, Fiester defines participation as "active enrollment," whereas attendance, which can be measured in a variety of ways (for example, daily, weekly, by activity), is generally an indication of the time youth spend in programs.[27] We extend this distinction to suggest that there is a participation equation: participation = enrollment + attendance + engagement. This equation proposes that attendance is a necessary but not sufficient component of participation; enrollment and attendance without engagement do not reflect true participation. True, youth cannot benefit from participation if they do not attend, but increasingly, as research in this chapter and elsewhere in the issue asserts, merely being there is not what makes real improvements in youth outcomes. Although there is no denying that providing a safe haven for youth in their nonschool hours is no trivial accomplishment, and this is a concern first and foremost for many families, we also know that OST programs can be stimulating, enriching environments where youth can do more than feel safe. They can learn, they can explore, and they can grow. But this rests on their engagement in the program. Being there keeps youth safe, but being engaged enables them to grow. Requisite to understanding engagement is articulating the program activities and features that encourage young people to be active participants.

The participation equation has implications for the evaluation of participation and its links to outcomes, necessitating the development of multiple indicators that capture information about access to programs, effectively recruiting youth into OST programs, and the nature and quality of the OST experience once enrolled. Although most participation research to date has focused on the single component of attendance, this chapter and this issue propose that to fully understand, and then intervene to improve, participation in OST programs, issues of access, enrollment, and engagement must be considered, and in the context of program quality.

A conceptual model of participation

The growing research base on the potential benefits of OST participation, coupled with recent evaluation research that indicates that low attendance is the norm at most OST programs, necessitates understanding of how to meaningfully engage youth in OST programs and activities and how to sustain that engagement. HFRP has developed a conceptual model of participation in out-of-school time, which is shown in Figure 1.1.

Figure 1.1. Harvard Family Research Project conceptual model of participation in out-of-school time

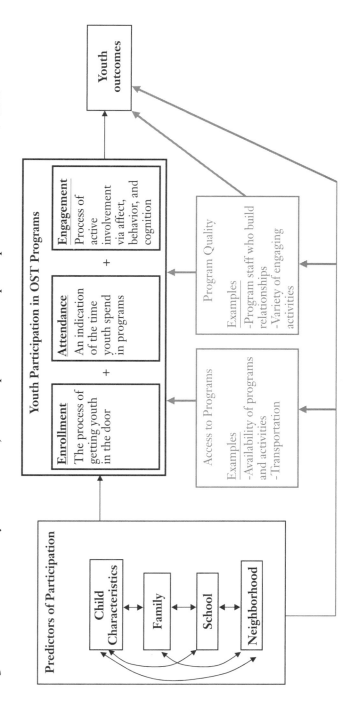

This model is based on scholarly theory, empirical research, knowledge gained from practitioners, and existing theories of change about how OST programs influence outcomes,[28] as well as the work of Daro and McCurdy on developing an integrated theory for parent involvement in family support programs.[29] It describes influences on youth participation in programs and potential outcomes of that participation.

The first half of the model proposes that the characteristics of children, families, schools, and neighborhoods together influence participation in OST programs. Examining multiple individual and contextual factors as predictors of participation is consistent with a long tradition in developmental research of acknowledging interactions between individuals and contexts. As in other disciplines, the importance of relationships between individuals and contexts has become a fixture of research on youth development. In their study of family processes in poor, urban communities, Furstenberg and colleagues stress the importance of simultaneously considering youth, their neighborhoods, schools, and family contexts.[30] The responsibility for youth outcomes cannot be placed solely on neighborhoods, schools, families, or children alone, but rather lies in the interaction of these contexts.

The second half of the model focuses on the relations between children's participation in OST programs and their social and academic outcomes.[31] In the center of the model is our participation equation: participation = enrollment + attendance + engagement.

The model illustrates the position that to truly reap the benefits of participation in OST programs, there must be a balanced equation that considers all three aspects of participation.

Enrollment

Enrollment is the act of getting youth in the door. Many factors contribute to enrollment, including the contextual predictors described in our model, program recruitment and retention strategies, and program quality features. In addition, we know that selection bias can influence program recruitment strategies as well as program implementation. Some youth are already predisposed to participate in OST programs, while others need more active recruitment efforts, taking into account the external forces at play to influence their decisions. The chapters in this issue contribute to our understanding of enrollment by examining promising recruitment strategies and program quality features, and pointing to the need for more intentional outreach to specific youth populations. Special attention in this issue is given to the cultural factors that promote or inhibit enrollment by specific ethnic groups. The issue also examines socioeconomic status and gender as key predictors of enrollment and subsequent youth outcomes.

Attendance

Attendance is generally an indication of the time youth spend in programs.[32] To date, many researchers and evaluators interested in measuring attendance have grouped youth into one of two categories: those who attend OST programs and those who do not. In some instances, such as the need to report average daily attendance for funding purposes, this is a sufficient indicator of attendance. However, while the yes-no groupings have been and will continue to be useful in our understanding of overall OST program participation, measuring attendance in such global terms glosses over critical information about how often youth attend programs (intensity, or "dosage"), how many years they attend (duration), whether they participate in one or several activities (breadth), and the level of concentration in any specific content area (depth). In order to understand the importance of attendance to youth outcomes, it is essential to collect attendance data using these more precise indicators. Only then can programs begin to establish realistic attendance goals that match the content of the program and the developmental stages of the participants. Some of the chapters in this issue examine why it is important to establish more meaningful and nuanced ways to measure attendance as well as practical strategies for how to do so.

Engagement

Of the three aspects of participation, engagement is the least researched yet perhaps the most critical component of participation. Although there is emerging research on the nature of engagement in OST (some of it presented in this issue), the literature on engagement in schools is further advanced and we can turn to it to better understand this component of the equation. Engagement in the school day involves both behaviors (such as persistence, effort, and attention) and emotions (such as enthusiasm, interest, and pride in success).[33] Just as attendance is a necessary but not sufficient component of participation, so too is motivation a necessary but not sufficient component of engagement. Engagement is not only motivation to be there; it is also being actively involved in cognitive and social endeavors that promote growth. Applied in an OST context, we know that many youth *do* attend OST programs, but the nature of their experiences, due to lack of interest on their part or lack of adequate programming structure or choice, or a combination, leaves them bored, disengaged, and not fully participating in the activities offered. We know that the context for engagement matters. Consistently, a core set of program features has been identified as key to youth engagement in OST programs: a sense of personal safety, relationships with caring adults, opportunities for leadership, opportunities for socializing with peers, and engagement in high-quality learning experiences. Some of the chapters in this issue tackle engagement in multiple ways, with the key hypothesis that engagement is a critical element of what youth need to succeed in OST programs: identifying key factors related to sustained participation in OST programs, understanding directly from youth the reasons that they do or do not participate in OST programs, applying what we know about school engagement to an OST context, and understanding how the differences between program and nonprogram participants relate to activities, emotions, and engagement.

Additional factors affecting the model

There are at least two additional and important components that influence the overall participation model as well as the participation equation: access to programs and program quality.

Without access to programs, the conversation about the relationship between participation and outcomes is moot. Yet we know that access to OST programs varies across gender, ethnicity, and income levels.[34] Across the country, communities are using geomapping to better understand and redistribute resource allocations. But there is more work to be done to help programs understand and address issues of access and, from a policy perspective, to help establish equitable distribution of access to quality non–school hour opportunities.

Research on child care[35] and feedback from OST practitioners and policymakers[36] speak to the importance of program quality (such as the practices used and relationships established by adult staff members) in the relations between participation and outcomes. Although some new work is under way to better understand the relationship between quality and outcomes (one is the Study of Promising After School Programs),[37] further research on quality is imperative in order to maximize the benefits of participation.[38]

The participation equation: Issues for research and practice

To fully understand the impact of OST programs on youth outcomes and implement programming that maximizes their impact, there must be a balanced participation equation. Any single component of the equation is necessary but not sufficient. Youth must enroll, for a sufficient length of time, in an engaging OST environment, to reap full benefits of participation. The chapters in this issue offer research-based program strategies to boost enrollment, increase attendance, and sustain engagement in OST programs and activities. Throughout the chapters, five key research and practice issues emerge that cut across participation and influence the equation:

• *Expectations for participation should vary by age of participants.* Research on the relationship between participation and outcomes demonstrates a developmental component to participation.[39] Programs for older youth need to understand that youth participate in multiple activities in their nonschool time and to truly understand the benefits of participation in any single program, program leaders and researchers need to understand the full complement of what older youth do after school, including "doing nothing" in safe places. A lighter dose of any single program may be sufficient for older youth, whereas consistent attendance in a single program may be better suited to elementary school–age participants. A related point is that programs for middle and high school youth need to set realistic attendance goals based on age, with expectations for fewer days in any single program as youth get older and want to explore more options and have the freedom to do so.

• *Expectations for participation should be established according to program goals and services.* Correlational studies suggest that higher levels of participation can lead to improved outcomes, but does this mean there is a threshold at which attendance matters to achieve these outcomes? Although research does not have the answer yet, we do know that the thresholds set need to be based on the program goals. For example, a program that intentionally seeks to improve academic performance through homework help will need to have consistently high levels of attendance intensity to result in the desired outcome of homework completion. However, it is possible that to yield social development skills such as leadership and responsibility, youth do not need to attend with the same intensity or frequency as a homework help session; instead, they need opportunities for relationship building and problem solving with peers and adults. However, whether a program is trying to improve homework completion or promote leadership skills, engagement in the program needs to remain high.

• *There is no single indicator for assessing participation, but understanding the components of participation can lead to stronger programs.* Related to the previous two points, the diversity of OST programming necessitates consideration of the goals and needs of individual programs when assessing participation. Although it is unlikely that the field will develop a single "dosage" measure that works for all programs, programs can and should collect meaningful participation data to feed into a system of accountability and program improvement. Reflecting on enrollment strategies and patterns of participation can help with program planning and ensure that programs are reaching their desired target populations. Furthermore, participation data should include assessments of engagement in program activities as well as documentation of successful enrollment strategies. Collecting information on the full range of participation components will serve to strengthen programs and help eliminate access barriers.

• *Understanding who participates and why will help our understanding of access issues.* Research, presented in this issue and elsewhere, is under way to understand the predictors of participation in order to target services better to those who need it the most.[40] Continuing to push on this line of research, including capturing the voices of youth about what they say is important to them, is critical to ensure equity in access to programs, especially for underserved and at-risk youth.

• *Program leaders and researchers need to take a systemic view of participation.* Organized OST programs are not the only places that children learn and grow in their nonschool hours. To fully understand participation and its impacts on learning and development, we must examine the totality of what children and youth do in their out-of-school time, including the important role of families. Only when we understand the full array of complementary supports for youth and their families can we begin to tease out the benefits of participation in specific programs.

Notes

1. Throughout this issue, the term *out-of-school time* (OST) is used to refer to a range of activities and programs that are offered to youth ages five to eighteen during the nonschool hours.

2. Afterschool Alliance. (2004). *America after 3 pm: A household survey on afterschool in America, Executive Summary.* Washington, DC: Author. Available at http://www.afterschoolalliance.org/press_archives/america_3pm/Executive_Summary.pdf.

3. Afterschool Alliance. (2004).

4. Duffett, A., & Johnson, J. (2004). *All work and no play?* New York: Public Agenda.

5. Mahoney, J. L. (2000). School extracurricular activity participation as a moderator in the development of antisocial patterns. *Child Development, 71,* 502–516; Mahoney, J. L., Eccles, J. S., & Larson, R. W. (2004). Processes of adjustment in organized out-of-school activities: Opportunities and risks. In G. G. Noam (Ed.), *After-school worlds: Creating a new social space for development and learning* (pp.

115–144). San Francisco: Jossey-Bass; Roeser, R. W., & Peck, S. C. (2003). Patterns and pathways of educational achievement across adolescence: A holistic-developmental perspective. In S. C. Peck & R. W. Roeser (Eds.), *Person-centered approaches to studying development in context* (pp. 39–62). San Francisco: Jossey-Bass.

6. Furstenberg, F. F., Cook, T. D., Eccles, J., Elder, G. H., & Sameroff, A. (1999). *Managing to make it: Urban families and adolescent success.* Chicago: University of Chicago Press.

7. Simpkins, S. (2003). Does youth participation in out-of-school time activities make a difference? *Evaluation Exchange, 9*(1), 2–3, 21. Available at www.gse.harvard.edu/hfrp/eval/issue21/theory.html.

8. Casey, D. M., Ripke, M. N., & Huston, A. C. (2004). Activity participation and the well-being of children and adolescents in the context of welfare reform. In J. L. Mahoney, R. W. Larson, & J. S. Eccles (Eds.), *Organized activities as contexts of development.* Mahwah, NJ: Erlbaum.

9. For a thorough review of the research that examines program participation and its relations to outcomes, see Simpkins, S., Little, P., & Weiss, H. (2004). *Understanding and measuring attendance in out-of-school time programs.* Cambridge, MA: Harvard Family Research Project. Available at http://www.gse.harvard.edu/hfrp/projects/afterschool/resources/issuebrief7.html.

10. Gambone, M. A., Klem, A. M., & Connell, J. P. (2002). *Finding out what matters for youth: Testing key links in a community action framework for youth development.* Philadelphia: Youth Development Strategies and Institute for Research and Reform in Education.

11. Little, P., & Harris, E. (2003). *A review of out-of-school time program quasi-experimental and experimental evaluation results.* Cambridge, MA: Harvard Family Research Project. Available at www.gse.harvard.edu/hfrp/projects/afterschool/resources/snapshot1.html; Mahoney, J. L., & Cairns, R. B. (1997). Do extracurricular activities protect against early school dropout? *Developmental Psychology, 33*(2), 241–253; Posner, J. K., & Vandell, D. L. (1994). Low-income children's after-school care: Are there beneficial effects of after-school programs? *Child Development, 65,* 440–456; Simpkins, S. D., Davis-Kean, P. E., & Eccles, J. S. (2004). *The role of activity participation and beliefs in high school math and science course selection.* Manuscript submitted for publication.

12. Eccles, J. S., & Templeton, J. (2002). Extracurricular and other after-school activities for youth. *Review of Research in Education, 26,* 113–180; Grossman, J. B., Resch, N. L., & Tierney, J. P. (2000). *Making a difference: An impact study of Big Brothers Big Sisters.* Philadelphia: Public/Private Ventures; Pettit, G. S., Laird, R. D., Bates, J. E., & Dodge, K. A. (1997). Patterns of after-school care in middle childhood: Risk factors and development outcomes. *Merrill-Palmer Quarterly, 43,* 515–538; Simpkins, S. D., Fredricks, J., Davis-Kean, P., & Eccles, J. S. (in press). Healthy minds, healthy habits: The influence of activity involvement in middle childhood. In A. Huston & M. Ripke (Eds.), *Middle childhood: Contexts of development.* Cambridge: Cambridge University Press; Vandell, D. L., & Shumow, L. (1999). After-school child care programs. *Future of Children, 9*(2), 64–80. Available at www.futureofchildren.org/usr_doc/vol9no2Art7done.pdf.

13. Murnane, R. (2004, July 9). *Teaching expert thinking and complex communication and making them fun: A role for after-school?* Paper presented at Getting

and Using Data to Improve Out-of-School Time Programs: Exploring Key Participation Issues, Harvard Family Research Project, Harvard University, Cambridge, MA.

14. It is unclear whether this is a causal relationship because youth and their parents determine their participation level. Thus, a participant with high program attendance may differ in several aspects from a participant with low attendance.

15. Simpkins, Little, & Weiss. (2004).

16. Kane, T. J. (2004). *The impact of after-school programs: Interpreting the results of four recent evaluations.* Working paper, W. T. Grant Foundation.

17. Kane. (2004); U.S. Department of Education, Office of the Under Secretary. (2003). *When schools stay open late: The national evaluation of the 21st-Century Community Learning Centers program, first year findings.* Washington, DC: Author. Available at www.ed.gov/pubs/21cent/firstyear/index.html.

18. After-school participation is consistently higher for elementary school students, whose parents have greater authority over their whereabouts during the after-school hours. The average participation rate for an elementary student in the national 21st CCLC evaluation was fifty-eight days. U.S. Department of Education. (2003).

19. Walker, K. E., & Arbreton, A.J.A. (with the Stanford University School of Education Research Team). (2004). *After-school pursuits: An examination of outcomes in the San Francisco Beacon Initiative.* San Francisco: Public/Private Ventures. Available at www.ppv.org/ppv/publications/assets/168_publication.pdf.

20. Grossman, J. B., Price, M. L., Fellerath, V., Jucovy, L. Z., Kotloff, L. J., Raley, R., & Walker, K. E. (2002). *Multiple choices after school: Findings from the Extended-Service Schools Initiative.* Philadelphia: Public/Private Ventures. Available at www.mdrc.org/publications/48/full.pdf; Grossman, J. B., Walker, K., & Raley, R. (2001). *Challenges and opportunities in after-school programs: Lessons for policymakers and funders.* Philadelphia: Public/Private Ventures. Available at www.ppv.org/ppv/publications/assets/120_publication.pdf; Kane. (2004). Walker, K. E., & Arbreton, A.J.A. (2001). *Working together to build Beacon Centers in San Francisco: Evaluation findings from 1998–2000.* Philadelphia: Public/Private Ventures. Available at www.ppv.org/ppv/publications/assets/118_publication.pdf.

21. Prenovost, J. K. E. (2001). *A first-year evaluation of after school learning programs in four urban middle schools in the Santa Ana Unified School District.* Irvine: University of California, Irvine. U.S. Department of Education. (2003). Weisman, S. A., & Gottfredson, D. C. (2001). Attrition from after school programs: Characteristics of students who drop out. *Prevention Science, 2*(3), 201–205.

22. Lauver, S., Little, P., & Weiss, H. (2004). *Attracting and sustaining youth participation in after school programs.* Cambridge, MA: Harvard Family Research Project.

23. Larson, R. W. (2000). Toward a psychology of positive youth development. *American Psychologist, 55,* 170–183.

24. Hansen, D. M., Larson, R. W., & Dworkin, J. B. (2003). What adolescents learn in organized youth activities: A survey of self-reported developmental experiences. *Journal of Research on Adolescence, 13,* 25–55.

25. Barber, B. L., Eccles, J. S., & Stone, M. R. (2001). Whatever happened to the jock, the brain, and the princess? Young adult pathways linked to adolescent activity involvement and social identity. *Journal of Adolescent Research, 16*, 429–455; Eccles, J. S. (1993). School and family effects on the ontogeny of children's interests, self-perceptions, and activity choice. In J. Jacobs (Ed.), *Nebraska Symposium on Motivation, 1992: Developmental perspectives on motivation* (pp. 145–208). Lincoln: University of Nebraska Press.

26. Simpkins, Little, & Weiss. (2004).

27. Fiester, L. (2004). *Afterschool counts! A guide to issues and strategies for monitoring attendance in afterschool and other youth programs.* Princeton, NJ: Robert Wood Johnson Foundation.

28. Miller, B. M. (2003). *Critical hours: Afterschool programs and educational success.* Dorchester, MA: Nellie Mae Education Foundation; Noam, G., Biancarosa, G., & Dechausay, N. (2002). *Afterschool education: Approaches to an emerging field.* Cambridge, MA: Harvard Education Publishing Group; Vandell, D. L., & Reisner, E. L. (2004). Investigating quality: The study of promising after-school programs. *Evaluation Exchange, 10*, 28–29.

29. Daro, D., & McCurdy, K. (2001, April). Parent involvement in family support programs: An integrated theory. *Family Relations, 50*, 113–121.

30. Furstenberg, F. F., Cook, T. D., Eccles, J., Elder, G. H., & Sameroff, A. (1999). *Managing to make it: Urban families and adolescent success.* Chicago: University of Chicago Press.

31. Little & Harris. (2003). Miller. (2003). Vandell & Reisner. (2004).

32. Fiester. (2004).

33. National Research Council and the Institutes of Medicine. (2004). *Engaging schools: Fostering high school students' engagement and motivation to learn.* Committee on Increasing High School Students' Engagement and Motivation to Learn. Board on Children, Youth, and Families, Division of Behavioral Sciences and Education. Washington, DC: National Academies Press.

34. Chapter Three, this volume.

35. NICHD Early Child Care Research Network. (2001). Non-maternal care and family factors in early development: An overview of the NICHD Study of Early Child Care. *Journal of Applied Developmental Psychology, 2*, 457–492.

36. Vandell & Reisner. (2004).

37. For more information about the Study of Promising After-School Programs, go to www.wcer.wisc.edu/childcare/des3.html.pdf.

38. For more information and resources on quality in OST programs, see the spring 2004 issue of the HFRP publication, *Evaluation Exchange*, dedicated to exploring issues of quality in OST. Available at http://www.gse.harvard.edu/hfrp/content/eval/issue25/spring2004.

39. Simpkins, Little, & Weiss. (2004).

40. See, for example, information on a new research project, *Individual and contextual predictors of out-of-school time activities*, at HFRP.org.

HEATHER B. WEISS *is the founder and director of the Harvard Family Research Project at the Harvard Graduate School of Education.*

PRISCILLA M. D. LITTLE *is the associate director of the Harvard Family Research Project and the project manager of HFRP's Out-of-School Time Learning and Development Project.*

SUZANNE M. BOUFFARD *is a research analyst at the Harvard Family Research Project and a doctoral candidate in developmental psychology at Duke University in Durham, North Carolina.*

Improving access to and interest in out-of-school-time programs is an important goal. A recent study examined the reasons that youth participated or not in programs, with a focus on the experiences of ethnic minority youth.

2

To participate or not to participate: That is the question

Lynne M. Borden, Daniel F. Perkins,
Francisco A. Villarruel, Margaret R. Stone

THERE HAS BEEN A GROWING interest in issues pertaining to how a young person chooses to participate (or not) in youth programs, both school based (for example, sports, drama, yearbook) and community based (for example, Boys and Girls Clubs, Scouts, 4-H, sports, faith-based programs). Scholars, youth workers, policymakers, national organizations, and funding agencies have repeatedly sought a deeper understanding of the influence of participation in youth programs on the developmental pathways of young people. One critical area for research is learning about the processes through which adolescents initiate their participation in programs and either persist or drop out, particularly for youth who are traditionally underserved by such programs, such as ethnic minority youth. Given the apparent benefits of activity participation, it is important to remove barriers and increase access and, equally important, to design programs of interest to youth in the contexts in which they live. To help understand these issues, this chapter

NEW DIRECTIONS FOR YOUTH DEVELOPMENT, NO. 105, SPRING 2005 © WILEY PERIODICALS, INC.

describes a qualitative study that examined youths' reasons for participating or not participating in out-of-school-time (OST) programs, with a focus on ethnic minority youth.

Why study participation among ethnic minority youth?

Growing evidence suggests important benefits for young people who participate in OST programs.[1] However, if the state of research is to advance, there must be a better understanding of how selection factors operate so that we can better assess the true effects of activities.[2] It is possible that youth with more preexisting assets or capacities are selected in to activities, or that they are subsequently more likely to benefit from and persist with activities than their peers with fewer advantages. Moreover, there can be factors beyond preexisting assets or capacities that have a bearing on young people's choices regarding potentially enriching activities. For example, if the decision to participate is based on external forces such as parents and peers instead of an individual's motivation, are the effects of the programming the same? Similarly, is there a differential impact of parental influence across context (rural, urban, suburban) as well as across race and ethnicity?

Understanding what influences young people's decision to participate is particularly salient for underserved youth populations. Youth workers and researchers have noted that ethnic minority youth, particularly those living in economically distressed communities, do not participate equally in youth programs[3] and have asserted that there is a need for more information to develop "culturally-sensitive approaches to engage un-served, under-served, and disenfranchised audiences."[4] The challenges and risks associated with low-income urban settings—high rates of unemployment, crime, violence, and lack of access to affordable housing and health services—contribute to the particular need that young people living in these environments have for structured youth programs.[5] Such factors, unfortunately, can also function as persistent barriers to participation for ethnic minority youth.[6] There is clearly a need to better understand the predictors of participating and dropping out among ethnic minority youth, and that is what this study sought to investigate.

The role of ethnicity in the choice to participate in youth programs

In one study of urban African American youth who attended activities at the YMCA or Boys & Girls Clubs, youth most frequently identified "fun" as the motivation for their participation.[7] The same study found that girls who participated in activities at Girls, Inc. (a national youth-serving organization that promotes the positive development of girls) more frequently cited the opportunity to learn things and to interact with caring adults at the program as the main motivations for participation. Passmore and French found in their Australian sample that the most important criteria for activities in leisure time were that they be freely chosen and that they be enjoyable.[8] Carruthers and Busser evaluated Boys & Girls Club programs in large cities in the Southwest and reported on the perceptions of youth participants, the majority of whom were African American or Latino and living below poverty levels.[9] A sense of safety and belonging, the acquisition of positive behaviors (for example, "staying out of trouble," "getting along with others"), and the development of competence and self-esteem were the three themes most frequently mentioned as benefits of participation.

The two most frequently mentioned reasons for participation by Latino youth attending youth programs in Chicago's West Town were that the programs provided a safe place and that the youth valued their relationships with program staff.[10] Latino, African American, and non-Latino youth interviewed at a teen center in Texas indicated that they participate because a teen center is a fun, safe place that provides something to do, opportunities for social interactions with peers, an escape from home, and a chance to learn healthy behaviors and achieve improved academic performance.[11] The same study asked youth to explain reasons teens did *not* participate in programs at the teen center. Frequently mentioned explanations were that they perceived the center as "boring" and that some youth might be involved in drugs and alcohol, which could keep them from participating.[12]

In a study of Extended-Service School programs (ESS), researchers evaluated sixty community-designed, school-based OST programs in twenty communities around the country.[13] The ESS Initiative was launched in 1997 to develop after-school programs in seventeen cities nationwide, each using one of four nationally recognized models of service delivery. Its evaluation found that one-third of participants identified themselves as African American and one-fifth as Latino. When asked why they did not attend the programs more often, the most frequent responses from the youth were that they had "other things to do," they were not interested in the activities, or their friends did not attend.

Few studies have considered the perceptions of youth regarding what factors motivate their participation in programs and what factors function as barriers to participation. Even fewer studies have examined the opinions of youth from various ethnic backgrounds. The study that follows, done by members of our research group, involved urban youth who identified themselves as Black/African American, Latino, Arab American, or Chaldean (ethnic people from the region now known as Iraq), and reported that they are active participants in some form of structured program for youth. These youth were asked to provide the researchers with ideas about why they and other young people in their neighborhoods and schools choose to participate or not to participate in community-based youth programs.

A qualitative study of ethnic minority youth

The goal of our study was to research youth representing the largest ethnic or ancestral identities in Michigan. The two largest ethnic populations in Michigan are black/African American and Latino.[14] Arab Americans are the third largest and fastest-growing ethnic group in Michigan, and southeastern Michigan is home to the largest population of Arab Americans in the United States.[15]

The region is also home to the largest population of Chaldeans in the United States.[16]

After target ethnicities were identified, the research team identified nine ethnic-oriented, community-based organizations (CBOs) that provided neighborhood-based OST programs for youth. The criteria for representative CBOs were that they serve one or more ethnic minority populations and provide services that include structured programs for youth living in an urban setting. Eight of the nine CBOs offered drop-in services for youth during the school year and summer.

Study participants were between the ages of nine and nineteen, participated in some type of organized youth programming, and identified their ethnicity as African American, Latino, Arab American, or Chaldean.[17] Participants were thirty-three females (median age fourteen years old) and forty-four males (median age thirteen years old), of whom over half reported that they attended the programs at least three times a week.

In the first phase of this study, we conducted eleven brainstorming sessions with youth using an adaptation of concept mapping analysis with Concept Systems methodology.[18] Concept mapping is a structured methodology that initially involves brainstorming, sorting, and ranking to develop a conceptual framework. Each session lasted about an hour and was audiotaped for transcription. One member of the research team acted as facilitator to direct the discussion, while a second member took written notes. The young people were asked two interview probes: (1) "One of the reasons young people take part in youth programs is . . . ," and (2) "One of the reasons other young people are NOT involved in youth programs is . . .".

Data analysis included a categorical survey to help reduce data to more manageable themes.[19] Analysis began by reviewing the large flip chart pages, all written notes recorded by the research team during and immediately after each youth meeting, and the written responses from participants. These first two sources were cross-checked by listening to all of the audiotapes in order to record direct quotations from the youth. Identity-concealing labels for participants were used in order to conserve anonymity, so only

gender, ethnicity, and study site are indicated. A total of 344 statements were recorded expressing reasons that young people participate in youth programs and 353 statements expressing reasons that
young people do not participate. These numbers reflect a great deal
of duplication because many of the statements were shared by
young people in multiple groups or repeated by several members
of the same group. Statements expressing reasons for participation
were sorted separately from the statements reporting barriers to
participation.

Reasons youth participate

The statements describing reasons youth participate in youth programs fall into four categories: how youth programs helped young
people stay off the streets, learn new things, avoid boredom, and
participate in enjoyable activities that are fun. Youth described the
youth programs as a way to keep out of trouble: "because you don't
want to be involved in street activities, because the streets don't do
anything but get you locked up." Other youth indicated that participating in these programs helped them learn new skills and gain
new knowledge. In addition, in every session, the short answer to
the question of participation was simply, "It's fun."

Although there was considerable consensus, reasons for participation varied by gender and ethnic group. African American
females indicated that the programs helped them to overcome shyness and develop confidence and self-esteem, giving them a way "to
prove that you can do something when someone said you can't."
African American males indicated that their involvement had to do
with staying "off the streets." Having fun was another frequently
mentioned reason for participation, and the youth also said that the
programs offered a chance to get away from home, "to get out
of your house, away from your parents, away from your chores,
and . . . away from your brothers and sisters."

Arab American females mentioned that youth programs were
fun and offered a way to keep "off the streets." Other reasons
that were most prevalent included the chance to develop personal skills and a chance to be involved in doing something
positive for the community. The teenagers explained that youth

programs "help make you outgoing and friendly . . . and you feel more connected to others . . . to the world." Arab American males mentioned that youth programs provided a safe alternative to the streets and helped keep people out of trouble, as well as providing homework assistance and help in learning new skills. One group participant explained, "After-school programs teach you how to do stuff so you get better at it, and they do it in fun ways."

Chaldean females mentioned homework assistance as a primary reason to attend youth programs. In addition to the four main topics consistently brought up by groups, they also stressed that the programs helped them learn English and gave them new opportunities to make friends. Chaldean males too mentioned that homework assistance and learning were among their main reasons for participation. One participant also described another important reason that was rarely mentioned aloud by male participants: "If you need help with something, not only schoolwork, but like drugs, or if a girl likes you, and you can talk to somebody here, like another girl or an adult, . . . they'll tell you what to do."

In addition to reasons brought up in other groups, Latinas mentioned that they particularly valued youth programs because they provided activities that were not available in school. Other reasons were the chance to learn about cultures and careers and to be involved in the community. Acceptance by peers and program staff was another reason. One Latina explained that people come to programs "because they want to be part of something." Latinos stated that the major reasons for participation were involvement in sports and other fun activities and the chance to avoid boredom.

Reasons youth do not participate

When participants discussed the reasons that their peers do not participate in youth programs, the similarities were less obvious between the genders and the ethnic groups. Four main reasons were mentioned by the participants: (1) youth were too busy or lacked time, (2) had other interests, (3) held negative opinions of the youth center, or (4) were constrained from participation by parents or guardians.

African American females indicated that major barriers had to do with competing interests and negative opinions of the youth center, held by both the participants themselves and their peers. The youth shared negative opinions that the programs were perceived as "boring" or "they think it's for little kids." For older youth, particularly those over age fifteen, the presence of younger children at the youth centers was described as a major deterrent. The teenagers also mentioned that the opinions of their peers could be a barrier to participation. Several participants explained that some youth programs were not popular, so "it's not all right to come—you might get teased." African American males also noted that the influence of peer opinions was one of the major barriers. Another perceived barrier most strongly voiced by African American males was the quality of program staff. The young men described programs to be avoided as those that were run by staff who do not relate well to young people.

Lack of time (often due to homework or babysitting) and lack of confidence were the most frequently mentioned barriers by the Arab American females. They reported that some females might not participate because of low self-esteem or "they think they can't do it . . . that it's hard." Peer pressure, in the form of negative opinions of others, was also mentioned. This group indicated that they were not allowed to participate in coed swimming, and some parents did not allow their daughters to go out at night. Arab American males also mentioned that their parents could prohibit them from participating, specifically in terms of work and study behaviors. One participant explained the priorities in his family: "I joined the football team, but my dad made me quit because I had to work. . . . My dad tells me school is more important than work, and work is more important than sports." The young men also mentioned that the negative opinions of peers were a major deterrent to participation for some of them.

Chaldean females noted that other youth were engaged in risky behaviors, which effectively prevented them from participating: "They think: why waste their time here when they could be out having fun, partying, smoking, doing drugs." The females voiced concern over safety as a barrier to participation, explaining that some youth "think it's dangerous because bad people are outside the building." Comments about parents were also made, similar to those made by Latina and Arab American females, regarding fears that the females would get involved with males. One Chaldean female said, "My mother won't let me [participate in some activities] because she worries about me getting into trouble with boys." Chaldean males explained that the major barriers were other interests that were taking up their time, such as sports or bike riding. Similar to their female counterparts, they also mentioned that their parents prevented them from attending programs because "parents are scared something bad might happen to their children."

Latinas mentioned two barriers repeatedly: they were unable to participate because they had to do chores at home, such as babysitting a younger sibling, and their parents did not allow them to participate: "Fathers are strict because they don't like their daughters to be around boys." One Latina elaborated: "Parents treat girls differently than boys." Latinos, not unlike African American males, mentioned that some youth do not attend youth programs because they are busy "doing drugs," "getting high," and "busy with their girlfriends." Other interests, such as watching television, were mentioned as reasons some youth stay away. The Latinos said that lack of information about the programs and lack of money for participating had prevented them from getting involved in the past. They also mentioned that shyness, as well as body image reasons, could be a barrier.

An in-depth look at the participation of Latino and Latina youth

Studying one group of minority youth in greater depth expanded this study by offering the opportunity to learn more about the participation of Latino and Latina youth.[20] The median age of these youth was sixteen years, and 60 percent of the participants were female.

These youth were asked to rate each of the youth-generated statements based on its personal importance to them. Each item was rated on a 1 to 5 scale with Likert-type responses, where 1 = "this isn't important to me" and 5 = "VERY important reason."

Latinos from the urban high school Latino club as well as youth who participated in the brainstorming sessions completed rating questionnaires. Eighty individuals rated the importance of the reasons youth participate, and seventy rated the importance of the reasons youth do not participate.

Notable differences emerged in how Latinas and Latinos rated the importance of the various reasons (see Table 2.1). These responses were compared to youth from families with different generational histories in the United States: youth who reported that they or their parents (or both) had immigrated to the United States and youth who indicated that their grandparents had immigrated to the United States, or their family had been in the United States for many generations. These two groups identified many of the same issues, but their rankings of these reasons were distinctive. Table 2.2 depicts the top five reasons for Latino youth to participate in youth programs by generational history.

Young people also rated the statements about why youth do not participate. There are again notable differences based on gender (see Table 2.3) and generational standing (see Table 2.4). It is interesting to note that Latinas and Latinos both rated statements describing "Home/school/work" constraints and "Lack money/transportation" as the top two reasons.

These in-depth qualitative studies offer insight into what influences young people to participate and what inhibits their participa-

Table 2.1. Ranking of the top five reasons youth chose to participate, by gender

Rank	All Latino Youth	Latinas	Latinos
1	Personal development/ confidence	Personal development/ confidence	Personal development/ confidence
2	Improve self/ community	Improve self/ community	Increase social life
3	Learn life skills	Emotional regulation	Learn life skills
4	Emotional regulation	Learn life skills	Improve self/ community
5	Safe haven/respite	Learn job skills	Safe haven/ respite

Table 2.2. Ranking of the top five reasons youth chose to participate, by generational status

Rank	Youth or parents moved to United States	Youth from families in United States at least since grandparents
1	Personal development/ confidence	Personal development/ confidence
2	Learn job skills	Increase social life
3	Safe haven/respite	Emotional regulation
4	Learn life skills	Improve self/community
5	Improve self/community	Learn job skills

Table 2.3. Cluster ranking of the top five reasons youth do not participate in youth programs

Rank	All Latino Youth	Latinas	Latinos
1	Home/school/work	Home/school/work	Home/school/work
2	Lack money/ transportation	Lack money/ transportation	Lack money/ transportation
3	Don't like people who run program	Family/religious priorities	Don't like people who run program
4	External constraints	Safety issues	External constraints
5	Safety issues	Peers not involved	Safety issues

Table 2.4. Cluster comparison by generation in the United States: Top five reasons youth do not participate in youth programs

Rank	Youth or parents moved to United States	Youth from families in United States at least since grandparents
1	Home/school/work	Home/school/work
2	Safety issues	Lack money/transportation
3	Don't like the people who run the program	Don't like the people who run the program
4	External constraints	Family/religious priorities
5	Lack money/transportation	External constraints

tion from the perspective of minority youth, and thus offer initial understanding of the influence of culture on these decisions. Clearly participation is not just dependent on a young person's understanding of the benefits of participation, but also on contextual variables such as resources, family, culture, religion, and outside responsibilities. The challenge is to offer programs that can be free of some of the barriers identified and provide opportunities that can more closely align with individuals' personal responsibilities.

In order to establish generalizability, the studies should be replicated across contexts. It can be assumed that similar patterns may exist among other panethnic groups (such as Asian and Middle Eastern) that comprise different ethnic and religious cultures, but further study is needed.

What we have learned

There is growing evidence that when young people participate in youth programs, they benefit from this experience. These experiences often offer young people the opportunity to build important life skills needed for a successful transition to adulthood, including the ability to organize tasks, use problem-solving strategies, and work collaboratively with others. Moreover, it has also been established that young people who participate in youth programs are less likely to engage in risk-taking behaviors and are more likely to be involved in voluntary-type activities as adults.

Although participation in youth programs is likely to benefit development, young people cannot determine whether to participate or not to participate if they do not have access to programs. Far too often, these programs do not exist in their schools or their communities. This is often true for young people who live in the inner city or in rural areas. The lack of access to programs can be clearly seen when communities map the location of youth programs. This mapping process often reveals that programs are located in close proximity to each other, so that some young people who live in the right neighborhood or town have multiple opportunities for engagement in a wide variety of activities with numerous programs, while other youth have few, if any, program choices.

In addition, young people are interested in more than programs that are fun. They are looking for well-run programs with high-quality staff who can provide them the opportunity to learn new skills and prepare them for the transition to adulthood, that is, a program based on a community youth development framework. Furthermore, programs must be designed to meet the needs of a particular audience. Perhaps a group of immigrant youth is in need of an opportunity to develop their English language skills through structured discussions and role-play in social interactions. Young people come from a wide variety of backgrounds and bring with them a wide variety of needs, interests, and skill levels that programs must address.

Key recommendations

Do I wish to participate or not to participate in this program? That is the question that young people ask themselves when considering a new opportunity. What, then, can be done to increase the likelihood that they will choose to participate? The following are recommendations for designing inclusive programs for young people:

- Clearly identify the audience that will be served by this program. Have you conducted a survey or examined local statistics to determine the number of youth who could participate in this program? Have you met with the young people to determine what they see as an important goal of the program? Do they have special needs, wants, or desires for this program?
  Have you not only identified minority youth in the area but determined their generational status?
- Design programs that offer young people the opportunity to build important life skills.
  Is your staff well trained and prepared to work with this particular audience?
  Is the program both interesting and challenging?
  Does the program have a logic model that clearly delineates the life skills the program will work on with each of its activities?
  Does the program allow time for peers to spend time together?
  Does it facilitate language development for young people who are immigrants?

- Design programs so that parents can be actively involved.
  Is the program designed to involve parents?
  Is the program designed to bring families together?
  Is there a focus on parental involvement?
- Include best practices in programs (see Table 2.5).[21]

Table 2.5. Best practice elements characteristic of effective youth development programs

Program Element	Explanation
Physical and psychological safety	Provides a safe haven both physically and emotionally.
Appropriate structure	Has clear rules, expectations, and responsibilities. Youth are involved in creating this structure.
Supportive relationships	Has adults involved in the program's activities and events. Through these activities and events, adults and youth are able to establish trust.
Opportunities to belong	Provides activities and events that foster friendships and provides youth with a sense of a positive group experience.
Positive social norms	Culture that governs behavior and daily interactions involves conventionally positive social norms.
Support for efficacy and mattering	Provides youth, both individually and in groups, the opportunity to be useful and to make a difference in their social worlds.
Opportunities for skill building	Develops skills and competencies through its activities and team-building experiences.
Active learning	Provides learning opportunities that are interactive, reflective, and engage multiple learning styles.
Opportunities for recognition	Sincerely acknowledges the contribution of youth.
Integration of family, school, and community efforts	Coordinates its efforts and communicates regularly with families and schools to ensure similar norms and expectations across settings.

Source: Adapted from Perkins, D. F., & Borden, L. M. (2003, April). Spider web analysis for a youth program. University Park: Penn State Cooperative Extension. Available at http://resiliency.cas.psu.edu/SpiderWeb.html.

- Continually evaluate the program.
  Have you interviewed not only those young people who currently participate but those who do not participate in your program? Have you carefully evaluated your program in the key areas?

Both program success and benefits to individuals depend on successful processes of recruitment and retention. As this review illustrates, choices regarding initial or continuing participation are likely to differ depending on a good person-environment fit between programs and their particular communities.[22] Because there is little doubt that out-of-school programs can have benefits for many different subpopulations of youth, the continuing challenge will be to provide programs that offer a good fit with the characteristics and interests of a broad range of potential participants.

Notes

1. Eccles, J., & Gootman, J. A. (2002). *Community programs to promote youth development.* Committee on Community-Level Programs for Youth, Board on Children, Youth, and Families, Commission on Behavioral and Social Sciences Education, National Research Council and Institute of Medicine. Washington, DC: National Academy Press.

2. Eccles, J. S., Barber, B. L., Stone, M. R., & Hunt, J. (2003). Extracurricular activities and adolescent development. *Journal of Social Issues, 59,* 865–889. Mahoney, J. L. (2000). School extracurricular activity participation as a moderator in the development of antisocial patterns. *Child Development,* 71(2), 502–516.

3. Brown, R., & Evans, W. P. (2002). Extracurricular activity and ethnicity: Creating greater school connection among diverse student populations. *Urban Education,* 37(1), 41–58; Davalos, D. B., Chavez, E. L., & Guardiola, R. J. (1999). The effects of extracurricular activity, ethnic identification, and perception of school on student dropout rates. *Hispanic Journal of Behavioral Sciences,* 21(1), 66–77.

4. U.S. Department of Agriculture Cooperative State Research, Education, and Extension Service. (2000). *The next agenda—National 4-H strategic plan 2000.* Washington, DC: U.S. Department of Agriculture; Bocarro, J. (2002). Moving beyond the walls: The need for youth outreach programs. *Parks and Recreation,* 37(3), 28–43; Carnegie Corporation of New York. (1992). *A matter of time: Risk and opportunity in the non-school hours, Task Force on Youth Development and Community Programs and Carnegie Council on adolescent development.* New York: Carnegie Corporation.

5. U.S. Census Bureau. (2000). Summary File 1 (SF 1), Matrix P8. *Census 2000.* Available at http://www.census.gov; Aneshensel, C. S., & Sucoff, C. A.

(1996). The neighborhood context of adolescent mental health. *Journal of Health and Social Behavior, 37*, 293–310; McLoyd, V. C., & Wilson, L. (1992). Telling them like it is: The role of economic and environmental factors in single mothers' discussions with their children. *American Journal of Community Psychology, 20*, 419–444; Schinke, S. P., Cole, K. C., & Poulin, S. R. (2000). Enhancing the educational achievement of at-risk youth. *Prevention Science, 1*, 51–60.

6. Villarruel, F. A., Montero Sieburth, M., Dunbar, C., & Outlay, C. W. (in press). Dorothy, there is no yellow brick road: The paradox of community youth development approaches for Latino and African American urban youth. In J. Mahoney, J. Eccles, & R. Larson (Eds.), *Organized activities as contexts of development: Extracurricular activities, after-school and community programs.* Mahwah, NJ: Erlbaum.

7. Gambone, M., & Arbreton, A. (1997). Safe havens: *The contributions of youth organizations to healthy adolescent development.* Philadelphia: Public/Private Ventures.

8. Passmore, A., & French, D. (2001). Development and administration of a measure to assess adolescents' participation in leisure activities. *Adolescence, 36*, 67–75.

9. Carruthers, C. P., & Busser, J. A. (2000). A qualitative outcome study of Boys and Girls Club program leaders, club members, and parents. *Journal of Park and Recreation Administration, 18*(1), 50–67.

10. Halpern, R., Barker, G., & Mollard, W. (2000). Youth programs as alternative spaces to be: A study of neighborhood youth programs in Chicago's West Town. *Youth and Society, 31*, 469–506.

11. Baker, D., & Hultsman, J. (1998). *Thunderbirds Teen Center program evaluation.* Available at http://rptsweb.tamu.edu/Faculty/Witt/conpubs/thunder.pdf.

12. Baker & Hultsman. (1998).

13. Grossman, J. B., Price, M. L., Fellerath, V., Juvocy, L. Z., Kotloff, L. J., Raley, R., & Walker, K. E. (2002). *Multiple choices after-school: Findings from the extended-service schools initiative.* Philadelphia: Public/Private Ventures.

14. U.S. Census Bureau. (2000).

15. Aswad, M. (2001). *Health survey of the Arab, Arab-American, and Chaldean American communities in Michigan.* Detroit: Michigan Department of Community Health-Division of Family and Community Health.

16. Aswad. (2001).

17. Chaldeans are an ethnic people who come from a region that is now Iraq. Chaldeans are Christians, and many have immigrated to the United States. The 2000 census reported 34,484 Chaldeans in Michigan, but estimates from social services agencies suggest that there are between 45,000 and 90,000 living in southeast Michigan. M. Fahkouri, personal communication, June 10, 2002.

18. Trochim, W. (1989). An introduction to concept mapping for planning and evaluation. *Evaluation and Program Planning, 12*, 1–16.

19. Rich, M., & Ginsburg, K. R. (1999). The reason and rhyme of qualitative research: Why, when, and how to use qualitative methods in the study of adolescent health. *Journal of Adolescent Health, 25*, 371–378. Borden, L. M., Perkins, D. F., Villarruel, F. A., Carleton-Hug, A., Stone, M., & Keith, J. (2004, March). *Challenges and opportunities to Latino youth development: Increas-*

ing meaningful participation in youth development programs. Manuscript submitted for publication.

20. Perkins, D. F., & Borden, L. M. (2003, April). *Spider web analysis for a youth program.* University Park: Penn State Cooperative Extension. Available at http://resiliency.cas.psu.edu/SpiderWeb.html.

21. Eccles & Gootman. (2002); Perkins & Borden. (2003).

22. McLaughlin, M. (2001). *Community counts: How youth organizations matter for youth.* Washington, DC: Public Education Network.

LYNNE M. BORDEN *is an associate professor and extension specialist of family studies and human development at the University of Arizona.*

DANIEL F. PERKINS *is an associate professor and an extension specialist of family and youth resiliency and policy at the Pennsylvania State University.*

FRANCISCO A. VILLARRUEL *is a university outreach and engagement fellow and a professor of family and child ecology at Michigan State University.*

MARGARET R. STONE *is an assistant research scientist in the Division of Family Studies and Human Development at the University of Arizona.*

Children's participation in organized out-of-school-time activities and the outcomes associated with those activities vary according to family social ecology and child characteristics.

3

Predicting participation and outcomes in out-of-school activities: Similarities and differences across social ecologies

Sandra D. Simpkins, Marika Ripke,
Aletha C. Huston, Jacquelynne S. Eccles

MANY ORGANIZED OUT-OF-SCHOOL-TIME (OST) activities provide enriching opportunities for children to interact with peers, build cognitive skills, develop relationships with mentors, and explore a variety of talents and leisure pursuits. A growing set of findings suggests that youth participation in OST activities is associated with academic achievement and overall well-being. Adolescents who participate in these activities have lower school absenteeism, are less likely to drop out, like school more, get better grades, and

This research was supported by grant HD17553 from the National Institute for Child Health and Human Development to Jacquelynne Eccles, Allan Wigfield, Phyllis Blumenfeld, and Rena Harold, and grants from the MacArthur Network on Successful Pathways through Middle Childhood to Eccles and Huston. We thank the principals, teachers, students, and parents of the cooperating school districts for their participation in this project.

NEW DIRECTIONS FOR YOUTH DEVELOPMENT, NO. 105, SPRING 2005 © WILEY PERIODICALS, INC.

are more likely to attend college than adolescents who do not participate in these activities.[1] Activity participation is also associated with positive social adjustment, such as low problem behavior, drug use, and loneliness.[2] This growing literature has greatly added to our knowledge concerning the role of OST activities in children's lives. Yet several questions remain. First, most research on this topic has been conducted with adolescents, but OST activities are an important component of many children's lives during the elementary school years as well. We need a deeper understanding of what leads younger children to participate in activities and whether the benefits associated with participation are greater for some children than for others.

In this chapter, we use data from two samples to examine whether there are gender and sample differences in participation in various organized activities and whether the relations of participation to adjustment are stronger for some subgroups than for others. Although children in both samples are of roughly the same age and report on similar measures of participation and outcomes, their family incomes, socioeconomic status, ethnicity, and neighborhoods are very different. The youth in the first study, Childhood and Beyond (CAB), come from largely white, middle-class families in urban, suburban, and rural Michigan, whereas those in the second study, New Hope, are from low-income families in Milwaukee who are primarily African American and Hispanic.

The majority of research on OST activity participation has focused on its relation to academic and social development, presumed to be consequences of participation, rather than on antecedents or predictors of participation. Understanding who participates can assist program directors in improving and sustaining youth involvement. We examine possible differences for children in the two social ecologies sampled by CAB and New Hope and differences between girls and boys.

Previous studies show differences in participation associated with family socioeconomic status (SES). Children from economically disadvantaged families spend more time in informal and unstructured activities compared to their more advantaged counterparts.[3] U.S. Census data show that only 3 percent of children ages six to fourteen living in poor families participated in organized sports, compared to 26 percent of children in more affluent families.[4] Conversely, children from more affluent families are more likely to be enrolled in lessons, organized sports, and clubs than are children from low-income families.[5] Low-income parents rely more on community centers and such national youth-serving organizations as the Boys & Girls Club and the YMCA as out-of-school arrangements.[6]

These SES differences may be a product of disparity in family resources (money to pay for fees, materials, and equipment), divergence in availability, differences in values, or other dissimilarities in family ecologies. Middle- and upper-income parents have more money to pay the costs of expensive enrichment programs, and they are more likely to have readily available transportation as well as the flexibility in work schedules to transport their children to practices, lessons, and events.[7] Youth in low-income families may have more restraints on their free time because of caregiver and household responsibilities that constrain the time they can spend away from home. Low-income neighborhoods and schools may have fewer activities available, and parents may have more concerns about safety or negative influences of the peers who will be involved. These circumstances may explain why children from low-income families are less likely to participate in most activities, particularly those that require substantial community, time, or monetary resources, such as sports.

Girls and boys also engage in different patterns of activities. A long research tradition has established gender differences in children's play styles, peer group size, and toy selection that may carry forward to children's choices about how they spend their time out of school.[8] For example, although the gender gap in sports is decreasing, boys still participate in more sports than girls do.[9] Girls participate in more faith-based and other types of activities than boys do.[10] With few exceptions, however, little work has systematically addressed gender differences in participation.

Relations between participation and developmental outcomes

Although most research shows that positive outcomes are associated with children's participation in activities, a handful of studies suggest that these relations vary depending on characteristics of the child, family, and activity. For instance, emerging research suggests that the impact of activity participation is larger for adolescents who are not doing well academically or socially than for those who are more successful.[11]

Children from low-income families are more likely to have behavioral and academic problems, which stem partly from the less cognitively stimulating and emotionally supportive qualities of these children's environments. Introducing enriching OST activities into the lives of low-income children may have a larger impact than it would for middle-class youth, who are more likely to have an enriching home environment, as well as access to enriching activities outside the home. For example, Marshall and colleagues found that elementary school children's involvement in an after-school program was associated with low levels of internalizing problems (such as depression and loneliness), but only for low-income children.[12] Few researchers, however, have examined whether the relationship between activity participation and children's developmental outcomes varies by families' SES levels.

Boys are also more likely than girls to have behavioral and academic problems, but there is little evidence about whether participation relates differently to developmental outcomes for males and females. The available findings are inconsistent. In some studies, participation in sports was positively associated with boys' grade point averages (GPAs)[13] but not with girls' GPAs. In another study, Gore and colleagues found that adolescents' sports involvement was positively linked to boys' and girls' GPAs.[14] We supplement this research by studying gender differences in the relations between activity involvement and a variety of child outcomes.

Different types of activities are likely to provide unique experiences and might therefore lead to divergent outcomes. Although children in formal after-school activities spend more time in inter-actions with peers, academic activities with adults, and enrichment lessons than children in other after-school care settings,[15] it is likely that children's experiences vary depending on the type of activity. For example, athletic teams and religious education classes provide different opportunities for cooperation and interactions with peers and adults. Research on adolescents shows that sports activities are associated with fewer feelings of depression, but there is no relation of depression to involvement in art, community service-type activ-ities, or school activities.[16] Although a handful of studies have exam-ined multiple activities, many studies on younger children focus on one or two specific activities or on total involvement rather than multiple endeavors. In this chapter, we incorporate a range of OST activities in order to gain a deeper understanding of children's involvement and of the outcomes associated with these activities.

This chapter focuses on differences in children's participation in activities based on family social ecology and child gender and how the relations between participation and outcomes vary based on family ecology, gender, and activity type.

The Childhood and Beyond Study: Overview and methods

The CAB study began in 1987 when children were in kindergarten, first, and third grades. This investigation includes data from three waves: wave 2 (when children were in first, second, and fourth grades; $n = 501$), wave 3 (second, third, and fifth grades; $n = 455$), and wave 4 (third, fourth, and sixth grades; $n = 393$). Children from these three waves cover a similar age range as the first wave of the New Hope data set, which is described in the next section. Children were initially recruited through their public school dis-tricts in four middle- and working-class communities near Detroit, Michigan. This sample is composed of primarily two-parent (90 percent), European American families with middle-class incomes (the 1990 annual income ranged from $10,000 to $80,000; median = $50,000 and $59,000). Data on children's OST activities were collected from parents, and data on children's outcomes were reported by teachers.

Children's activities

To examine children's OST activity participation, parents listed up to twenty after-school activities, programs, and classes in which their child participated during the previous year. They were given a list of 117 activities from which to choose, but they could also list activities not on the roster. For each activity listed, parents described how many weeks their child participated in the previous year and how many hours per week their child participated in the activity while he or she was involved (1 = less than one hour per week, 4 = three to six hours per week, 7 = more than twenty hours per week). Parents also listed whether the activity was part of a formal, organized group; an informal, unorganized group; or both. Activities that were classified only as part of an informal, unorganized group were deleted from further analysis.

Using the activity data provided by parents, we created five activity groups, or types, to match the New Hope data set. Participation in each type of activity was defined by the average time the child spent in it each week across the year. The activity groups and types are as follows:

Sports included forty-one physical fitness and athletic activities.

Art lessons included seventeen activities, such as drama, painting, playing musical instruments, and singing.

Recreation and community center activities included three activities (day or overnight camps, general after-school programs, and other community activities).

Club and youth group activities included three activities: YMCA; scouting and similar groups, such as Brownies and Indian Girls; and church social groups.

Religious activities reflected children's participation in religious education classes. This category differed the most from the New

Hope data. In the New Hope study, religious activities included religious services and religious education classes.

Children's developmental outcomes

At wave 4 (spring 1990 when children were in third, fourth, and sixth grades), teachers rated how well children were performing in math and reading compared to how well the teacher believed they could perform (1 = far below ability, 7 = to maximum of ability). Also at wave 4, children reported their feelings about their academic abilities (that is, their academic self-concept). Teachers rated the likelihood of children's delinquent behavior in adolescence. One question, for example, asked, "How likely do you think it is that this child will use drugs during his/her adolescence?" The answers ranged from 1 (not at all likely) to 7 (very likely).[17]

The New Hope Project

The second sample for this study is part of a larger sample of low-income, primarily single-mother families who participated in the New Hope Project, an antipoverty demonstration program designed to enable families to move out of poverty through employment. New Hope participants were recruited from July 1994 to December 1995; adults with incomes at or below 150 percent of the poverty threshold were eligible. They were randomly assigned to a control group or to a New Hope program group that was eligible for income supplements, subsidized health care and child care, and case management if they worked at least thirty hours per week. If job searches were unsuccessful, community service jobs were available.[18]

This investigation includes data from children who were part of the Child and Family Study (CFS) sample, which included families of all 745 sample members who had one or more children between the ages of thirteen months and ten years eleven months at the time of random assignment. Up to two children in each CFS family were identified as focal children to be studied. Data for this study were collected from surveys administered to parents, focal children, and their teachers, where applicable. Parents were predominantly single (90.4 percent); 56.8 percent were African American, 26.6 percent were Hispanic, 13.1 percent were non-Hispanic white, and 3.5 percent were Native American. The proportion of boys and girls in this sample was roughly equal.

Children's mean participation levels in activities are presented for all children ages six to twelve for whom we have complete data (N = 541). However, in order to match the ages of children in the CAB (middle-class) study, analyses of the associations between activity participation and academic and social outcomes are restricted to children ages nine to twelve (N = 277).

Children's activities

Parents reported how frequently their children participated in lessons, sports with a team and/or coach, clubs and youth groups, and religious classes and events, and how often they attended recreation or community centers during the previous year using a five-point scale (1 = never, 2 = less than once a month, 3 = about every month, 4 = about every week, 5 = about every day). We then computed a mean score for structured activity participation.

Children's developmental outcomes

Children's academic performance was assessed with the Academic Subscale of the Social Skills Rating System (SSRS), on which teachers rated how well children were performing compared to their classmates using a five-point scale (1 = lowest 10 percent, 5 = highest 10 percent).[19] As with the CAB study, children's academic motivation was assessed. Whereas CAB measured children's academic self-concepts, New Hope measured children's academic expectations. Children ages nine to twelve reported how sure they were that they would complete high school (1 = not at all sure, 5 = very sure). As a parallel to CAB's measure of delinquent behavior, we analyzed parents' responses to the externalizing subscale of the Problem Behavior scale on the SSRS, using a five-point scale (for example, "is aggressive toward other people/objects"; 1 = never, 5 = all the time).[20]

Findings

Study results revealed that children's participation and the associated outcomes differed based on child characteristics and social ecologies.

Children's participation in activities

We examined both the percentage of children who participated in the various activities and the intensity of their participation (the frequency and amount of time spent). Figure 3.1 shows the percentage

Figure 3.1. Percentage of children who participated in various activities in CAB and New Hope

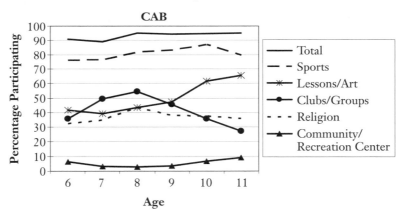

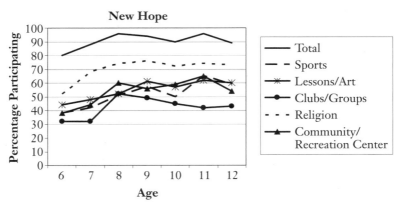

of children in the CAB study and the New Hope study who participated in various activities from ages six through twelve.

Children's participation varied based on the study and type of activity. The percentage of children participating in lessons and club/youth groups is similar across both samples. Some of the most notable differences between the two samples occur in sport, recreation/community center, and religious activities. As others have found,[21] children from middle-class families in CAB were more likely to participate in sports and less likely to go to community/recreation centers than the low-income children in New Hope.

In comparison to CAB, fewer New Hope children participated in sport activities. Specifically, at different ages, 75 to 85 percent of CAB children participated in sports, whereas only 40 to 60 percent of children in New Hope participated in sports. Fewer than 10 percent of CAB children participated in recreation/community center activities compared to 40 to 60 percent of New Hope children. More New Hope children participated in religious and recreation/community center activities. Participation rates for religious activities may have been lower in CAB than New Hope because the CAB questionnaire item contained only participation in religious education classes, whereas the New Hope questionnaire item included both participation in religious education classes and service attendance.

In wave 4 of CAB (when children were in third, fourth, and sixth grades), children also reported how much time they generally spent each week in religious services or doing religious activities. In contrast to the parents' report presented in Figure 3.1, 66 to 72 percent of CAB children reported spending time in religious activities, which is more consistent with parents' reports in New Hope (50 to 75 percent).

Another interesting comparison between the two studies is the pattern of participation across ages. In New Hope, the percentage of children participating in various activities generally increased with age, but in both samples, there are decreases in the percentage engaging in club/youth group activities after age eight (more pronounced in CAB). In CAB, the increases in art lesson participation were almost the mirror image of the decreases in club/youth group participation. The three other activities—sport, religious, and recreation/community center—appear fairly stable across time in CAB.

Participation patterns also differed across gender. In both studies, a higher number of girls participated in art/lessons than boys. Gender differences in sports participation depended on children's age. Younger boys (ages seven to nine in CAB and age nine in New Hope) were more likely to participate in sports than girls, but by age ten in CAB and age eleven in New Hope, there were no gender differences in sports participation. There were no gender differences in religious participation at any age in either study. The findings for club/youth groups and recreation/community centers were mixed. For the middle-class youth of CAB, club/youth groups and recreation/community center participation were similar for boys and girls. In New Hope, eight-year-old girls spent more time than boys did in clubs/youth groups; however, at ages eleven and twelve, the reverse was true: boys at ages eleven and twelve spent more time in recreation/community centers than did girls in New Hope.

The amount of time in activities is presented in Figure 3.2. Comparisons across CAB and New Hope are a little more challenging with this indicator of participation, as the scales differed across studies. CAB children's participation is indexed in hours per week. Participation of New Hope children has the following scale: 1 = never, 2 = less than once a month, 3 = about every month, 4 = about every week, 5 = about every day. In CAB, children spent more time in sport and art activities than in other activities, particularly during mid- and late elementary school. The time children spent in other activities remains relatively low at each grade level. Like children in CAB, children in New Hope spent a great deal of time in sports (it was the second most frequent activity), but they spent even more time in religious activities.

There were also some significant differences in the amount of time spent in activities based on gender.[22] Girls spent more time in art and lessons than did boys in both studies. Boys at seven, eight, and eleven years of age in CAB and New Hope spent significantly more time in sports than did girls. There were generally

Figure 3.2. Mean participation intensity across various activities in CAB and New Hope

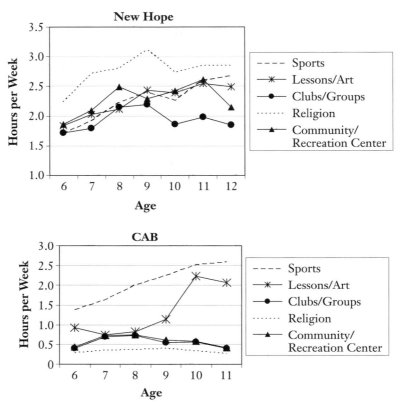

Note: In the CAB figure, means represent average hours of participation per week, averaged across the calendar year. In New Hope, means can be interpreted using the following scale: 1 = never, 2 = less than once a month, 3 = about every month, 4 = about every week, 5 = about every day.

no differences by gender for time spent in religious activities. The findings for clubs/youth groups are mixed: in New Hope, girls at younger ages (eight, nine, and ten) participated more frequently in clubs and youth groups than boys, while at ages eleven and twelve, the reverse was true. New Hope boys participated in recreation and community centers more frequently than girls did at ages six, eleven, and twelve. In CAB, boys and girls generally participated for similar amounts of time in recreation/community and club/youth group activities.

It is worth noting some differences between the two indicators of participation. For example, in CAB, although the percentage of children participating in sports remained steady as children aged (Figure 3.1), the time youth spent in sports increased across time (Figure 3.2). In addition, although the percentage of CAB children participating in club/youth group and religious activities differed from recreation/community center activities, the time youth spent in these three activities was similar (Figure 3.2). In New Hope, however, the two indicators of participation showed relatively similar patterns.

What does activity participation predict, and for whom?

To examine the relations of participation to children's develop-ment, we split youth into three groups based on the amount of time they spent in activities: (1) none, (2) low (less than one hour per week in CAB, less than or about once a month in New Hope), and (3) high (one hour or more per week in CAB, about every week or every day in New Hope).[23] Significant results from these analyses are organized by outcomes. Within each analysis, we examined the possibility of different associations for boys and girls. We could not do direct statistical comparisons of CAB and New Hope because the measures were somewhat different.

Academic performance

Children's academic performance varied by their participation in several activities. The children in CAB and New Hope who par-ticipated most frequently in sports and art/lessons (the high-participation group) had higher school performance than those who did not participate at all. New Hope children who had high participation in community/recreation centers also had higher school achievement than those who did not participate at all. CAB children who participated at high levels in club/youth groups, sports, or art/lessons outperformed children who participated at low levels in the same activities. Across all of these activities, CAB and New Hope children who participated at the high levels had higher academic performance than children who did not participate and sometimes had higher performance than youth who participated at low levels in the same activity in the CAB sample.

Academic beliefs

Children's beliefs about their academic abilities or their academic self-concept did not typically differ based on their activity participation in CAB. In the New Hope sample, participation in sports and recreation/community centers predicted expectations to complete high school. The children who participated in sports at low or high levels had higher expectations than those who did not participate at all. The children who participated at high levels in recreation/community centers had higher expectations than those who did not participate at all. Overall, however, there was not a strong link between participation and academic beliefs.

Problem behavior

In both studies, children's delinquent or problem behavior differed only based on participation in sports activities. Children's problem behavior did not vary based on participation in lessons, religious, recreation/community center, or club/youth group activities in CAB or New Hope. In CAB, boys and girls who participated in sports at high levels were rated by teachers as less likely to be delinquent in adolescence than youth who participated at low levels. Interestingly, high participators were not significantly different from nonparticipants in terms of teachers' expectations for delinquent behavior. In New Hope, children who participated in sports at high levels had lower levels of problem behaviors than those participating at low levels or nonparticipants.

Sex differences in relation to participation to outcomes

In each analysis, we tested gender differences in the relations between activity participation and child outcomes. In CAB there was only one case in which this happened: girls who participated in sports at high levels had significantly higher academic self-concepts than boys who participated in sports at high levels and than girls who did not participate in sports. With one exception in CAB, relations between participation and outcomes were similar for boys and girls. In New Hope, there were four cases in which the associations between participation and outcomes were different for boys and girls; in all of these, the association was stronger for boys than for girls. Specifically, participation in art/lessons and recreation/ community centers significantly predicted higher school achievement for boys but not girls, and sports and recreation/community center participation predicted educational expectations for boys but not for girls. The number of significant differences by gender is small, particularly in the case of CAB. With a few exceptions, the relations between participation and child outcomes were similar for boys and girls.

Participation and outcomes across two social ecologies

The findings from this investigation underscore some important messages. The patterns of activity participation for children in the two social contexts we investigated were quite different. Youth in CAB participated in more sports activities, and more New Hope children attended recreation/community centers and religious activities. These patterns are consistent with earlier findings comparing children from different SES levels, but these two samples differed in many ways: average income, ethnic group, area of the country, and types of neighborhood, to mention only a few. With that caution, we speculate that low-income families take advantage of religious institutions and local recreation and community centers more than the middle class families who enroll their children in lessons and sport teams because the former are more affordable and these types of activities are more readily available and easier to access in their communities.

We also compared boys' and girls' activities, finding some evidence for sex-typed activity content, which replicates and extends earlier findings.[24] Compared to girls, boys participated more in sports and less in art/lessons. There were no gender differences in involvement in the other types of activities sampled, suggesting that recreation/community centers, clubs/youth groups, and religious activities appeal to both boys and girls.

Despite the different levels of participation and the divergent social ecologies, the relations of participation to achievement and behavior were similar across the two samples. In both studies, participation was associated with favorable outcomes. The difference emerged in the comparison group. In CAB, children who participated most frequently had better outcomes than youth who participated at low levels and sometimes youth who did not participate. In the New Hope data, however, the differences consistently occurred between youth who participated at high levels and youth who did not participate at all. This may have emerged because the middle-class youth in CAB who are not involved in a particular activity are likely to be involved in something else. Thus, the comparison between youth in CAB who participate at high levels or not at all may actually be a comparison between youth who participate at high levels in activity A versus youth who participate at high levels in various other activities. New Hope children may have had fewer opportunities to participate in activities. In many studies, researchers and evaluators only compare youth who participate in activities (regardless of the amount of time they spend in these activities) with those youth who do not participate. If we had made this type of comparison only, we would have missed most of the significant differences in the middle-class CAB sample.

We expected that activity participation would be more strongly related to developmental outcomes in the New Hope sample because these children are more at risk for low academic performance and high behavioral problems. The results across the two samples, however, were highly consistent. Sports participation was associated with high achievement and low levels of problem or delinquent behavior in both samples; it also predicted high educational expectations for the New Hope children. Our results suggest that activity participation is linked with similar outcomes for both groups of youth.

The five activity categories we sampled had different patterns of relations to children's school performance and behavior, as have the few previous studies that included a variety of activities.[25] For both samples, participation in sports was a consistent predictor of good school performance and low behavioral problems. Sports also had the highest participation rates and intensity in the CAB sample, but that was not true in New Hope. Some activities may have had little impact because children did not participate in them very often, but the only very low rate occurred for recreation and community centers in CAB. The reasons for positive associations with sports and weak or nonexistent associations with other activities are not clear. In a sample of older children, one might guess that low achievers are selected out of sports by "no pass, no play" rules, which mandate that youth maintain a certain grade point average in order to participate in sports; however, that is not likely in elementary school. The next stage of research on out-of-school activities should address the processes by which activities play a role in children's development.

Notes

1. Eccles, J., & Barber, B. (1999). Student council, volunteering, basketball, or marching band: What kind of extracurricular involvement matters? *Journal of Adolescent Research, 14,* 10–43; Eccles, J. S., & Templeton, J. (2002). Extracurricular and other after-school activities for youth. In W. G. Secada (Ed.), *Review of research in education* (Vol. 26, pp. 113–180). Washington, DC: American Educational Research Association; Marsh, H. W. (1992). Extracurricular activities: Beneficial extension of the traditional curriculum or subversion of academic goals? *Journal of Educational Psychology, 84,* 553–562; Marsh, H. W., & Kleitman, S. (2002). Extracurricular school activities: The good, the bad, and the nonlinear. *Educational Review, 72,* 464–514; Simpkins, S. D., Davis-Kean, P. E., & Eccles, J. S. (2004). *The role of activity participation and beliefs in high school math and science course selection.* Manuscript submitted for publication.

2. Eccles & Barber. (1999); Marsh & Kleitman. (2002); Posner, J. K., & Vandell, D. L. (1994). Low-income children's after-school care: Are there beneficial effects of after-school programs? *Child Development, 65,* 440–456.

3. Medrich, E. A., Roizen, J., Rubin, V., & Buckley, S. (1982). *The serious business of growing up: A study of children's lives outside school.* Berkeley: University of California Press; Posner, J. K., & Vandell, D. L. (1999). After-school activities and the development of low-income urban children: A longitudinal study. *Developmental Psychology, 35,* 868–879.

4. Smith, K. (1997, Spring). *Who's minding the kids? Child care arrangements.* Current Population Reports, P70–86. Washington, DC: U.S. Census Bureau.

5. Hofferth, S. L., Brayfield, A., Deich, S., & Holcomb, P. (1991). *National child care survey*. Washington, DC: Urban Institute Press.

6. Halpern, R. (1999). After-school programs for low-income children: Promises and challenges. *Future of Children, 9*(3), 81–95; Pettit, G. S., Laird, R. D., Bates, J. E., & Dodge, K. A. (1997). Patterns of after-school care in middle childhood: Risk factors and development outcomes. *Merrill-Palmer Quarterly, 43*, 515–538.

7. Posner & Vandell (1999).

8. Maccoby, E. E. (1998). *The two sexes: Growing up apart, coming together*. Cambridge, MA: Harvard University Press.

9. Eccles & Barber. (1999); Posner & Vandell. (1999); Shann, M. H. (2001). Students' use of time outside of school: A case for after school programs for urban middle school youth. *Urban Review, 33*, 339–356.

10. Shann. (2001). Youniss, J., McLellan, J. A., Su, Y., & Yates, M. (1999). The role of community service in identity development: Normative, unconventional, and deviant orientations. *Journal of Adolescent Research, 14*, 248–261.

11. Mahoney, J. L. (2000). School extracurricular activity participation as a moderator in the development of antisocial patterns. *Child Development, 71*, 502–516. Mahoney, J. L., & Cairns, R. B. (1997). Do extracurricular activities protect against early school dropout? *Developmental Psychology, 32*, 241–253; Roeser, R. W., & Peck, S. C. (2003). Patterns and pathways of educational achievement across adolescence: A holistic-developmental perspective. In S. C. Peck & R. W. Roeser (Eds.), *Person-centered approaches to studying development in context* (pp. 39–62). San Francisco: Jossey-Bass.

12. Marshall, N. L. Coll, C. G., Marx, F., McCartney, K., Keefe, N., & Ruh, J. (1997). After-school time and children's behavioral adjustment. *Merrill-Palmer Quarterly, 43*, 497–514.

13. Holland, A., & André, T. (1987). Participation in extracurricular activities in secondary school: What is known, what needs to be known? *Review of Educational Research, 57*, 437–466; Yin, Z., Katims, D. S., & Zapata, J. T. (1999). Participation in leisure activities and involvement in delinquency by Mexican American adolescents. *Hispanic Journal of Behavioral Sciences, 21*, 170–185.

14. Gore, S., Farrell, F., & Gordon, J. (2001). Sports involvement as protection against depressed mood. *Journal of Research on Adolescence, 11*, 119–130.

15. Posner & Vandell. (1994).

16. Barber, B. L., Eccles, J. S., & Stone, M. R. (2001). Whatever happened to the jock, the brain, and the princess? Young adult pathways linked to adolescent activity involvement and social identity. *Journal of Adolescent Research, 16*, 429–455; Gore et al. (2001).

17. Academic self-concept was an eight-item scale; reliability was .79. The reliability of the two-item scale on children's performance was .85. The reliability of the delinquency scale was .93.

18. See Brock, T., Doolittle, F., Fellerath, V., & Wiseman, M. (1997). *Implementation of a program to reduce poverty and reform welfare*. New York: Manpower Demonstration Research Corporation.

19. Gresham, F., & Elliot, S., (1990). *Social skills rating system.* Circle Pines, MN: American Guidance Service.

20. Gresham & Elliott. (1990).

21. Hofferth et al. (1991); Smith (2002).

22. Gender differences were tested with independent *t*-tests. All tests discussed were statistically significant at least at $p < .05$ for all comparisons in CAB and New Hope.

23. Analysis of covariance (ANCOVA) was used to examine the associations between participation intensity and children's outcomes. In the CAB ANCOVAs, three variables were included as controls: child cohort, family income, and the highest educational attainment across parents. The control variables in the New Hope analyses were child age, family income, parent education, experimental/control group status, and ethnicity. The independent variables in each analysis were children's gender and activity participation. A separate ANCOVA was computed for each outcome and activity. Results that were statistically significant at least at $p < .10$ are discussed.

24. Eccles & Barber. (1999); Posner & Vandell. (1999); Shann. (2001).

25. Barber et al. (2001); Holland & André. (1987); Ripke, M., & Huston, A. C. (2003, July). *Does structured activity participation promote positive psychological and academic outcomes for low-income children during middle childhood and adolescence?* Paper presented at the Building Pathways to Success: Research, Policy, and Practice on Development in Middle Childhood, Washington, DC.

SANDRA D. SIMPKINS *is an assistant professor in the Department of Family and Human Development at Arizona State University.*

MARIKA RIPKE *is the project director of Kids Count Hawai'i at the University of Hawai'i at Manoa.*

ALETHA C. HUSTON *is the Pricilla Pond Flawn Regents Professor of Child Development and the associate director of the Population Research Center at the University of Texas at Austin.*

JACQUELYNNE S. ECCLES *is the Wilbert McKeachie Collegiate Professor of Psychology, Women's Studies and Education, as well as a research scientist at the Institute for Social Research at the University of Michigan.*

Out-of-school-time programs can increase youth participation using a set of promising strategies and a school and community-wide commitment to implement them.

4

Recruitment and retention strategies for out-of-school-time programs

Sherri C. Lauver, Priscilla M. D. Little

IF OUT-OF-SCHOOL-TIME (OST) programs are to achieve success in promoting positive youth development and learning, they must attract young people and maintain their consistent participation and long-term attendance. It is generally perceived that recruitment can be difficult, especially as youth grow older. A commentary on several recent large program evaluations observed that youth attend OST programs either irregularly or attend for only a brief period of time before they quit.[1] Many OST practitioners seek ways to maximize enrollment through effective recruitment strategies, increase frequency of participation, and ensure retention in OST programs, so that the multiple potential benefits of these programs are realized.

The importance of active youth participation in OST programs has been well documented in the literature; however, effective strategies for increasing participation have been given far less attention. Although there is no single best strategy to attract and sustain youth participation, there are some promising approaches that work. Here, we propose a set of research-derived strategies to

NEW DIRECTIONS FOR YOUTH DEVELOPMENT, NO. 105, SPRING 2005 © WILEY PERIODICALS, INC.

increase youth enrollment, improve program participation, and ensure long-term retention in OST programs.

Information for this chapter was obtained from a thorough review of the OST evaluation literature as well as structured telephone interviews with the directors of two project-oriented, academically based OST programs.[2] Evaluation research available in the Harvard Family Research Project's Out-of-School Time Program Evaluation database was reviewed to offer information on youth recruitment and sustainability in OST programs.[3] Of the sixty-four evaluation summaries available in the database at the time of writing this chapter, more than half of the studies reported at least some information or analysis of participation in OST programs.[4]

Elements of program quality critical to recruitment and retention

Ultimately, program quality is the critical framework on which all other issues regarding recruitment, participation, and retention hang. Without a quality program, efforts to recruit and retain youth are futile. Based on a review of the evaluation literature, however, it appears that three features are especially salient to a discussion about recruitment and retention:[5]

- A sense of safety and community, both physical and psychological
- Committed program staff who develop supportive relationships with youth
- Challenging, age-appropriate, and fun program activities

Each of these aspects of program quality, as it relates to successful recruitment and retention of youth, is described below.

Ensure participants' physical and psychological safety

In many urban areas, young people and their caregivers consistently state concern about safety as an issue that prevents or discourages them from attending OST programs. Successful programs often cite safe forms of transportation as essential for high attendance.[6] Programs that find ways to provide transportation, whether by bus, van, or "buddy systems" of walkers, discover that it is worth the extra effort and expense.

Participants' psychological safety must also be ensured. Young people need to trust that the adults who supervise them make safety their first commitment. No matter how likeable the staff or intriguing the activities, youth who perceive that an OST program is ruled by bullies or gangs will not enroll in the program or will drop out after a short period of participation. Furthermore, families will not feel comfortable entrusting their children to a program where they do not feel that safety can be ensured.

Hire committed program staff who make real connections with participants

A key finding of the San Francisco Beacons Initiative (SFBI) evaluation was the importance of staff to programs.[7] Positive relationships with OST staff members, along with a variety of interesting activities, were significantly associated with long-term participation. When youth are happy with their OST program, they describe it as a family. They develop a trusting relationship with the OST staff members and feel cared about;[8] in turn, these relationships improve the participants' likelihood of staying in the program.[9] Successful programs concentrate on building strong bonds between staff and new members within the first few months. Successful programs also employ staff members with varied expertise and interests who share the ability to connect to children and youth through humor, kindness, and support.

Engage participants with age-appropriate activities that offer breadth and depth

High-quality OST programs provide experiences that promote cognitive, social, emotional, physical, and cultural development. While many program activities are driven by staffing and physical resources, staff members should make efforts to offer a choice of activities and greater freedom than youth have during the school day. Consensus is emerging among OST stakeholders that after-school hours should not be "more school," and many advocate that school-based programs should attempt to differentiate themselves from, and not merely act as a continuation of, the school day.

A recent evaluation of several promising OST programs suggests that there is considerable diversity in the activities offered in programs. In fact, the best programs typically combine various types of activities.[10] In a recent review of promising practices in after-school, researchers found a variety of activities offered across elementary and middle school settings. For example, in elementary school OST programs, evaluators observed homework assistance programs, while middle school programs offered tutoring or helped participants to work on study skills and test preparation.[11] Performing arts, arts and crafts projects, and reading and math enrichment programs were common in both the elementary and middle grades. Sports and fitness were also offered to participants of all ages.

Recruitment strategies

Recruitment is best viewed as a process driven by "visibility, accessibility, and appeal."[12] Common recruitment strategies include flyers, announcements on school intercoms, open house events, and teacher referrals. However, low enrollment in OST programs (see Chapter One, this volume) suggests that these strategies may not be the most effective in getting youth in the door. A review of the evaluation literature reveals several promising strategies that go beyond the usual recruitment efforts to increase program enrollment.

Match program content and scheduling to participants' needs

A needs assessment or a study of the neighborhood, school, and community's OST options provides relevant background information to attract new youth to an OST program and minimizes the duplication of services within a community. In addition, a program that offers activities not readily available elsewhere may attract more participants.

In a recent evaluation of an OST recreation program in Philadelphia, both boys and girls participating in the evaluator's focus groups reported that there were few opportunities to participate in artistic activities, music, or dance during the program. The program director was able to respond by hiring a dance instructor two days a week and providing arts and crafts activities three days a week.[13] Enrollment immediately rose among females, who continued to participate regularly in the dance program. Intentional programmatic decisions about activities based on a needs assessment will help programs to attract and retain new participants.

Older youth may participate in OST programs only when they are offered a flexible schedule and can sign up for particular days or times, or can drop in for certain activities. Programs such as The After-School Corporation (TASC) have responded to teens' desire for flexibility by allowing them to check in with the OST program on the days when they are participating in a TASC-approved internship.[14] Organizing the program into eight-week blocks of various activities may also increase participation because it allows youth to participate on a periodic basis when they may have fewer outside activities. Other programs, including the Beacons Initiative and the Boys & Girls Clubs of America (BGCA), extend center hours to late evenings to allow for greater participation among youth who are involved in other afternoon activities.[15]

Many in the OST field are rapidly responding to teens' lack of interest in OST programs.[16] The directors of the After School Matters program in Chicago learned that teens desire opportunities to develop marketable skills, learn about careers, and contribute to the community. With this in mind, they designed a program to address those goals.[17] Based originally on an OST arts program, it reinvented teen OST programs through a citywide venture that provides older teens an apprenticeship with a working professional in one of four career areas (arts, sports, technology, and communications). The apprenticeships also include a stipend for participants. The combination of an innovative, practical program that addresses the needs of teens and a creative recruitment strategy using a colorful, hands-on, and engaging Web site has led to the involvement of twenty thousand teens.[18]

Drop-in programs or rolling admission policies (which mean that there are no fixed start and end dates) are two additional options for recruiting youth. One large program has found rolling admission to be a successful method for recruiting at-risk families.[19] Youth who quickly respond to a request to participate may be more motivated or advantaged than others, thereby creating selection bias. To allow all youth to participate on some level, the BGCA provides drop-in recreation centers and structured prevention and educational programs.[20]

Demonstrate the importance of participation to youth and their families

Establishing a connection between participation and a brighter future is a critical first step to recruiting youth and their families into OST programs.[21] During recruitment, staff should emphasize how the program will help youth develop the skills needed for the workplace or college. For example, three-quarters or more of the teens involved in Boys & Girls Clubs in Boston and New York City reported grade improvements, assistance with college applications, and help learning how to find and obtain a job while participating in their OST program.[22] These reported outcomes can be turned into selling points for OST programs.

Programs also need to make a strong case to parents of the benefits of involvement in OST.[23] Program practitioners may particularly need to convince parents, who may be dissatisfied with the school or the neighborhood, that the OST program will offer a high-quality alternative to unstructured activities.[24] The benefits of such programs include homework help and tutoring, socialization and new friendships, physical fitness activities, engagement with the arts, and associations with positive peers and caring adults to foster a child's positive development. In many urban communities, the OST program may be one of the few places where children have exposure to the arts and a chance to be physically active.

Reach out directly to youth and their families

Telephone calls and home or community visits to youth and their parents are an effective means of increasing local interest in OST programs and hence recruitment. Staff in the SFBI report that word of mouth is the best form of program advertising. Several of the sites involved in the Extended-Service Schools evaluation used recruitment strategies that were intended to be less stigmatizing to young people than referrals. For example, they visited public housing complexes to meet and greet youth and parents.[25] Other program staff members reached out to youth in the halls, before and after school on school grounds, and in school lunchrooms to raise interest in the program.[26] Other programs offer picnics or pizza parties at the beginning of the year for interested youth.

Youth participants in OST programs are often the most effective recruiters or ambassadors and can take on new leadership responsibilities through this role.[27] Youth may shun OST programs because they believe that the activities will not interest them, that they will be treated like children, or that they are places for troubled youth and those not doing well in school. Current program participants may offer an honest account of program activities and dispel other youths' misperceptions, leading to enhanced recruitment.

Recruit in peer circles

In a study of promising practices in after-school programs, researchers identified supportive relationships among participants as one of the key factors common across successful after-school programs.[28] In another recent study of 150 youth attending BGCA, friendships within the program significantly predicted participation.[29] In other words, when a youth's friends attended BGCA, those friends were more likely to participate.

Roughly half of the participants in the New York City Beacons Initiative stated that all or most of their friends attend Beacon Centers.[30] The evaluation of SFBI and a report on YouthBuild USA graduates also stressed that friendships are important motivators of participation.[31] In the 21st Century Community Learning Center (21st CCLC) evaluation, almost 80 percent of the nonparticipating youth reported that they would be more likely to attend a 21st CCLC after-school program if their friends were going too.[32] In an evaluation of teen programs in BGCA, Herrera and Arbreton found teen recruitment to be more successful when youth were recruited in peer circles or small groups. However, they caution against recruiting very large groups because all the members tend to quit together if one member stops attending.[33]

Although there is little information in the program evaluation literature about ways to increase participation by recruiting groups of friends or helping youth make new friends in the OST program, it appears to be an effective way to increase youth participation in OST programs. It may be worthwhile to spend time recruiting youth leaders because they may be more likely to bring their friends into the program. Incentives such as opportunities to help in the decision making about program activities and operations may be a useful recruitment strategy for these youth leaders.

Make a special effort to recruit at-risk youth

At-risk youth are those with a higher likelihood of school failure, who live in socially disorganized communities or have troubled family lives, who use drugs or alcohol or have peer drug models, and who have higher levels of school absences.[34] These are the youth considered most at risk who are least likely to sign up for OST programs and are significantly more likely to drop out of programs.[35] Despite this, they are also the youth most likely to benefit from OST programs.[36] Perhaps even a minimum level of participation may be important for these youth. Studies of the neediest participants in Upward Bound and Los Angeles's Better Educated Students for Tomorrow Program revealed that these youth made significantly greater academic gains than other participants and youth not participating in the evaluation.[37]

School-based OST programs have successfully involved at-risk youth by working closely with teachers to identify and encourage them to participate, earmarking a certain number of program slots for hard-to-reach children, and hiring staff members who demonstrate an ability to relate well to these youth.[38]

SFBI has been successful in reaching at-risk youth. Participants are more likely to be of lower socioeconomic status and demonstrate lower academic achievement than their nonparticipating counterparts.[39] SFBI attributes its success in recruiting at-risk youth to program staff who make efforts to build relationships with existing school staff who can refer the neediest students to them. In fact, Beacon Centers are provided specific funds to hire case managers who will work closely with the youth referred by schools for their poor behavior or other problems. In both cases, their emphasis on working with at-risk youth leads to an increase in teacher referrals.

Strategies to enhance regular participation and long-term retention

High-quality OST programs understand that benefits remain dependent on engaging children and youth to stay involved in programs over time. In a longitudinal study of one thousand elementary students and forty-three hundred middle school students involved in OST programs, evaluators found that many students do not return to programs after having attended a program the previous year.[40] Recognizing the need for sustained participation, programs employ a range of retention strategies.

Provide a clear message that attendance is important

Whether flexible schedules or a five-day-a-week schedule are offered, participants need to understand the expectations for their attendance and behavior in an OST program. Staff must continue to reinforce the connection between frequent participation and a brighter future. One way to communicate the importance of regular attendance is by setting explicit standards for youth and parents of high attendance in the program. This standard should be based on what appears to be the minimum level of attendance needed to achieve positive outcomes. Programs whose participants attend regularly often ask them to make a written commitment to the program and stick to it. At A Company of Girls, a theater-based OST arts program in Maine, girls and their parents attend an orientation and make a decision about whether they can commit to the schedule and demands of the program. This attendance policy may be effective because it is publicized and understood by program staff, participants, and families; is well aligned with program goals; and is designed to encourage rather than punish behavior.[41]

Certainly, youth should be asked to register for and make a commitment to OST activities that require a skilled instructor or facilitator and expensive equipment. If participants must register for these activities, limited program funds will not be wasted and instructors can properly prepare for their activities.

Conveying a clear message that attendance is important also involves caring, involved staff members who make youth feel that they are valued by staff and are missed when they are not present. It is every staff member's responsibility to be welcoming. Maintaining high levels of attendance could be as simple as greeting students as they leave their school buildings and asking them if they are planning to attend the program. Staff should make it clear that they want and expect youth to attend, even if it means seeking them out to make that connection.

If attendance begins to slip, some programs establish an early intervention plan for youth whose participation begins to decrease. When an attendance problem arises, a staff member is responsible for establishing immediate contact with youth and families through telephone calls or home visits.

The BGCA programs in New York City also offer an orientation for new teen participants to ease their concerns about the program and their safety there. The orientation has an added benefit of increasing long-term retention by helping new enrollees to feel comfortable in their new environment and by helping youth establish strong relationships with the program's staff.

Set realistic goals to promote regular attendance

While it is important to establish and articulate the importance of regular attendance, program practitioners must be realistic about the commitment most young people can make to an OST program. Programs need to consider multiple factors, such as program goals and participants' level of need, age, and interest, when setting programmatic attendance goals. Asking young people to attend five days a week appears to work best when these expectations are explicit to both youth and parents and attendance is monitored. Furthermore, these policies are more effective with elementary participants.[42]

It is especially important for programs reaching out to older youth (ages eleven to eighteen) to acknowledge that external factors contribute to low levels of attendance. Teens have many demands on their time—work, homework, caring for siblings—and program staff have little control over these issues. When program staff have some information about teens' commitments outside the program, it will help them manage their stakeholders' expectations for participation.[43] In addition, there are cultural differences in the choices that Latino and African American youth make about participation in OST programs, and these differences need to be factored into expectations about program attendance (see Chapter Two, this volume).

Balance academic activities with other leisure activities

Academically-based OST programs have some difficulty recruiting and retaining youth, especially middle and high school youth, whose parents have greater difficulty mandating where they spend their out-of-school time. Educational activities tend to have lower rates of attendance than do arts, recreation, or leadership activities in many OST programs.[44] Even academically successful students may not wish to regularly attend OST programs that are simply an extension of the school day. Many OST programs serving older youth hope to walk the fine line between becoming more school-like while providing for participants' other developmental needs and interests. But because these programs are voluntary, they need to be considerate of youth's many interests. OST academic activities or homework assistance may be more easily tolerated if there are exciting activities available.

Some programs attempt to disguise academic activities by embedding them within project-oriented activities, such as a play that participants write and produce themselves. In an evaluation of low-income children's participation in after-school literacy programs, Halpern suggests that keeping children engaged in academic curricula during OST time can be accomplished through a sufficient choice of high-interest materials displayed in an attractive and organized manner; encouraging participation among older youth with reading and writing activities focused on students' individual experiences and their relationships to texts; linking reading activities with related field trips; and involving games and group-oriented activities that introduce more socialization and fun into activities.[45] In sum, interested stakeholders need to continuously monitor the balance of educational and other activities to retain students.

Provide incentives for regular participation and long-term retention

Many programs offer youth incentives to boost their participation. Offering programmatic rewards such as the chance to participate in a desirable activity such as karate or gymnastics is one incentive to promote consistent attendance at homework sessions.

Younger children in a program funded by the Bresee Foundation earn points for participating in various activities. Later they can redeem points for school supplies, candy, or games.[46] Some programs, especially those geared toward high school youth, offer additional financial incentives for participation in OST programs. Presumably they offer these incentives to offset the costs of the lost opportunity for paid work. Since 2000, the After School Matters program in Chicago has offered paid apprenticeships during the school year and summer for youth ages fourteen and older. The stipends are based on the youth's experience in the program; for example, youth participating in their first summer program are paid $400 and the following summer receive $675. By the age of sixteen, they receive an hourly wage of $5.15. Moreover, these youth are working with professionals in fields such as technology, the arts, and communication. The executive director of the program notes that stipend programs are expensive but very important because they imply that work by the young people is valued and important.[47]

The Children's Aid Society Carrera-Model Teen Pregnancy Prevention Program offered younger teens three dollars per hour and older teens minimum wage for hours spent participating in a job club or on entrepreneurial or community-service projects. The teens' participation averaged sixteen hours a month, or four hours per week.[48] Perhaps even more important, about 70 percent of the original program participants followed for the evaluation study were still involved in the program at the end of the third year. The director of the program states that it is difficult to identify a single influence on attendance, but financial issues are important when working with older teens.[49] Perhaps the incentives help youth to learn the important concept of connecting work with money, an especially important lesson in communities where poverty, unemployment, and crime may be commonplace.

The use of incentives deserves greater attention as a strategy for improving youth's OST regular and long-term program participation. Given the costs, it may be worthwhile to evaluate this strategy as an enhancement to an existing program prior to implementing it on a larger scale.[50]

Keep teens involved with opportunities for leadership opportunities, community service, and paid employment

More than two-thirds of teens in a YMCA-sponsored nationally representative survey stated that they would be interested in participating in academic, leadership, and community service activities after school if they were available.[51] Although teens continue to express interest in programs, participation typically plummets when they reach the age of fifteen or sixteen.[52]

Teen programs that sustain interest and have positive effects for teens often include employment or service-learning (community service).[53] About one-third of teens (sixteen and seventeen year olds) in low-income communities work for pay, and many more are interested in paid employment. Older teens want greater independence by making money and taking on adult responsibility, and they may have the very real burden of contributing to their family's income. Some OST programs attract teens and meet their needs by offering job clubs, assistance finding work, or internships with local employers.[54] Other programs successfully blend academic activities and employment into intensive summer programs.[55] Chicago's After School Matters program, offering paid apprenticeships, has revitalized youth involvement in OST programs and resulted in sustained involvement over time.[56]

Service-learning activities are another option to keep youth inspired and interested.[57] Youth at the seventeen schools participating in a national evaluation of Learn and Serve America, a school-based initiative, spent on average seventy hours per year participating in volunteer service, and youth in some sites spent more than two hundred hours in these activities. More than 90 percent of the participants were satisfied with their service-learning experience.

Leadership opportunities are a third important motivator for retaining teens in OST programs. Geoffrey Canada, president and CEO of the Harlem Children's Zone, advocates that leadership opportunities in an OST program for teens, called TRUCE, promote the development of "leaders who are also positive role models."[58] Rewards for effective leadership, such as opportunities to travel to teen conferences or other places, are especially effective for developing leadership skills and enhancing long-duration retention.[59] Several community-based organizations have developed leadership training programs to enhance youth interest and retention. In a study of three national organizations serving youth (BGCA, Girls Incorporated, and the YMCA) program evaluators found that all three offered leadership activities.[60] If attendance is used as some approximation of youth interest and engagement, then the attendance data from these programs demonstrate that adolescents participated more frequently in programs that had a leadership component.[61] Not only do these programs enhance regular participation, they likely also have a positive impact on long-term retention.

Valuable lessons from evaluation

The valuable lessons presented in this chapter were gleaned from reviewing implementation evaluations, and this underscores the importance of continuing to collect information that will inform and improve participation in OST programs. Although it is unlikely that every OST program will employ all the strategies suggested here, some strategies, such as helping youth and their families understand the benefits of participation, are critical first steps to attract and sustain youth participation. Furthermore, it is clear from the evaluation literature that employing a range of strategies shows promise in boosting recruitment and participation in a variety of OST programs. Identifying the key features of programs that make them attractive to students and sustain their engagement for a sufficient length of time will serve to promote the long-term positive benefits of programs for all who participate.

Notes

1. Granger, R. C., & Kane, T. (2004, February 18). Improving the quality of after school programs. *Education Week*, pp. 52, 76. Available at www.edweek.org/ew/ewstory.cfm?slug=23granger.h23.

2. Interviews conducted with the program directors of A Company of Girls in Portland, Maine, and Youth Document, in Durham, North Carolina.

3. The Harvard Family Research Project database contains profiles of OST program evaluations, which are searchable on a wide range of criteria. It is available in the OST section of the HFRP Web site at www.gse.harvard.edu/hfrp/projects/afterschool/evaldatabase.html.

4. For more information on the programs for this chapter, see Lauver, S., Little, P., and Weiss, H. (2004). *Attracting and sustaining youth participation in out-of-school time programs.* Cambridge, MA: Harvard Family Research Project.

5. Other features of program quality are opportunities to belong; positive social norms; support for efficacy and mattering; appropriate structure; and integration of family, school, and community efforts. See Eccles, J., & Gootman, J. A. (Eds.). (2002). *Community programs to promote youth development.* Washington, DC: National Academy Press. Available at www.nap/edu/catalog/10022.html.

6. O. Bowman, personal communication to S. Lauver, October 9, 2003; B. Lau, personal communication to S. Lauver, October 5, 2003.

7. Walker, K. E., & Arbreton, A.J.A. (2004). *After school pursuits: An examination of outcomes in the San Francisco Beacon Initiative.* San Francisco: Public/Private Ventures. Available at www.ppv.org/ppv/publications/assets/168_publication.pdf.

8. McLaughlin, M. (2000). *Community counts: How youth organizations matter for youth development.* Washington, DC: Public Education Network. Available at www.publiceducation.org/pdf/communitycounts.pdf; Miller, B. M. (2003). *Critical hours: Afterschool programs and educational success.* Brookline, MA: Nellie Mae Education Foundation; Warren, C., Feist, M., & Nevarez, N. (2002). *A place to grow: Evaluation of the New York City Beacons. Summary report.* New York: Academy for Educational Development. Available at scs.aed.org/grow.pdf; Wright, D. (2004). *White paper on attendance and retention.* Somerville, MA: YouthBuild Academy for Transformation.

9. Wright, D. (2003, July). Improving attendance and retention. *From the field: News for and from HUD Youthbuild programs,* 22–23.

10. Forum for Youth Investment. (2003a). *Policy commentary #2: High school after school: What is it? What might it be? Why is it important?* Washington, DC: Forum for Youth Investment. Available at www.forumforyouthinvestment.org/comment/ostpc2.pdf.

11. Vandell, D. L., Reisner, E. R., Brown, B. B., Pierce, K. M., Dadisman, K., & Pechman, E. M. (2004, February). *The study of promising after school programs: Descriptive report of the promising programs.* Washington, DC: Policy Studies Associates.

12. Walker & Arbreton. (2004).

13. Lauver, S. C. (2002). *Assessing the benefits of an after-school program for urban youth: An impact and process evaluation.* Unpublished doctoral dissertation, University of Pennsylvania Press.

14. Forum for Youth Investment. (2004), p. 2.

15. Grossman, J. B., Price, M. L., Fellerath, V., Jucovy, L. Z., Kotloff, L. J., Raley, R., & Walker, K. (2002). *Multiple choices after school: Findings from the Extended-Service Schools Initiative.* Philadelphia: Public/Private Ventures. Available at www.mdrc.org/publications/48/full.pdf; Herrera & Arbreton.

16. Walker, K. E., Grossman, J. B., & Raley, R., with Fellerath, V., & Holton, G. I. (2000). *Extended Service Schools: Putting programming in place.* Philadelphia: Public/Private Ventures. Available at www.ppv.org/ppv/publications/assets/147_publication.pdf.

17. Anderson-Butcher, D., Newsome, W. S., & Ferrari, T. M. (2003). Participation in Boys and Girls Clubs and relationships to youth outcomes. *Journal of Community Psychology,* 31(1), 39–55.

18. Forum for Youth Investment. (2004, February). High school: The next frontier for after school advocates? *Forum Focus,* 2(1). Available at www.forumforyouthinvestment.org.

19. Forum for Youth Investment. (2004).

20. Forum for Youth Investment. (2004).

21. Wright. (2004).

22. Herrera & Arbreton. (2003).

23. Afterschool Alliance. (2004). *America after 3PM: A household survey on afterschool in America: Key findings.* Washington, DC: Author. Available at www.afterschoolalliance.org/america_3pm.cfm.

24. Wiseman, A. (2002, Spring). Neighborhood narratives: Learning about lives through conversations, writing, and photographs [Special Issue]. *Penn GSE Perspectives on Urban Education, 1*(1).

25. Grossman, J. B., Walker, K., & Raley, R. (2001). *Challenges and opportunities in after school programs: Lessons for policymakers and funders.* Philadelphia: Public/Private Ventures. Available at www.ppv.org/ppv/publications/assets/120_publication.pdf.

26. Lauver. (2002); Walker et al. (2000).

27. McLaughlin. (2000).

28. Vandell et al. (2004, February).

29. Anderson-Butcher et al. (2003).

30. Warren et al. (2002).

31. Walker & Arbreton. (2004); Wright. (2003).

32. U.S. Department of Education. (2003). *When schools stay open late: The national evaluation of the 21st Century Community Learning Centers program.* Washington, DC: Author. Available at www.ed.gov/pubs/21cent/firstyear/index.html.

33. Herrera & Arbreton. (2003).

34. Lauver. (2002). Weisman, S. A., Soule, D. A., Womer, S. C., & Gottfredson, D. C. (2001). *Maryland after school community grant program: Report on the 1999–2000 school year evaluation of the phase 1 after school programs.* College Park: University of Maryland.

35. Herrera & Arbreton. (2003); Olsen, D. (2000). *Twelve-hour school days? Why government should leave afterschool arrangements to parents.* Washington, DC: Cato Institute. Weisman et al. (2001).

36. Huang, D., Gribbons, B., Kim, K. S., Lee, C., & Baker, E. L. (2000). *A decade of results: The impact of the LA's BEST after school enrichment program on subsequent student achievement and performance.* Los Angeles: UCLA Center for the Study of Evaluation. Available at www.lasbest.org/learn/uclaeval.pdf; Myers, D., & Schirm, A. (1999). *The impacts of Upward Bound: Final report for phase 1 of the national evaluation.* Washington, DC: Mathematica Policy Research.

37. Huang et al. (2000); Myers, D., & Schirm, A. (1999). *The impacts of Upward Bound: Final report for phase 1 of the national evaluation.* Washington, DC: Mathematica Policy Research.

38. Forum for Youth Investment. (2003b). *Quality counts.* Washington, DC: Forum for Youth Investment, Impact Strategies. Available at www.forumforyouthinvestment.org/focus/focusv1i1jul03.pdf; Grossman et al. (2002); Walker & Arbreton. (2004).

39. Walker & Arbreton (2004).

40. Dynarksi, M. James-Budumy, S., Moore, M., Rosenberg, L., Deke, J., & Mansfield, W. (2004). *When schools stay open late: The national evaluation of the 21st Century Community Learning Centers program: New findings.* Washington,

DC: U.S. Government Printing Office. Available at http://www.ed.gov/ies/ncee.

41. Railsback, J. (2004). *Increasing school attendance: Strategies from research and practice.* Portland, OR: Northwest Regional Educational Laboratory. Available at www.nwrel.org/request/2004june/attendance.pdf.; Bowman. (2003).

42. Grossman et al. (2002).

43. Fiester, L., with Policy Studies Associates. (2004). *A guide to issues and strategies for monitoring attendance in afterschool and other youth programs.* New York: After School Project.

44. U.S. Department of Education. (2003); Walker & Arbreton. (2004).

45. Halpern, R. (2000). The promise of after school programs for low-income children. *Early Childhood Research Quarterly, 15*(2), 185–214.

46. Fiester. (2004).

47. Forum for Youth Investment. (2004).

48. Philliber, S., Williams Kaye, J., Herrling, S., & West, E. (2002). Preventing pregnancy and improving health care access among teenagers: An evaluation of the Children's Aid Society–Carrera Program. *Perspectives on Sexual and Reproductive Health, 34*(5), 244.

49. M. Carrera, personal communication to S. Lauver, October 20, 2003.

50. Shirk, M. (2004, November). Pay-as-you-go youthwork. *Youth Today.*

51. YMCA of the U.S.A. (2001). *After school for America's teens: A national survey of teen attitudes and behaviors in the hours after school.* Chicago: Author. Available at www.ymca.net/pdf/executivesummary.pdf.

52. YMCA of the U.S.A. (2001); Sipe, C. A., & Ma, P., with Gambone, M. A. (1998). *Support for youth: A profile of three communities.* Philadelphia: Public/Private Ventures.

53. Successful programs include the Teen Outreach Program, Learn and Serve America, CASCM, the Quantum Opportunities Program, and the four models in Extended-Service Schools Initiative. National Research Council and Institute of Medicine. (2002). *Community programs to promote youth development.* Washington, DC: National Academy Press. Available at www.nap.edu/catalog/10022.html; Hollister, R. (2003). *The growth in after school programs and their impact.* Washington, DC: Brookings Roundtable on Children, Brookings Institution. Available at www.brook.edu/views/papers/sawhill/20030225.pdf; Kirby, D. (2001). *Emerging answers: Research findings on programs to reduce teen pregnancy.* Washington, DC: National Campaign to Prevent Teen Pregnancy; Sawhill, I. V., & Kane, A. (2003). Preventing early childbearing. In I. V. Sawhil (Ed.), *One percent for the kids: New policies, brighter futures for America's children.* Washington, DC: Brookings Institution.

54. CASCM and the Quantum Opportunities Program offer these services. Forum for Youth Investment. (2004).

55. Shapiro, J. Z., Gaston, S. N., Hebert, J. C., & Guillot, D. J. (1986). *The LSYOU project evaluation.* Baton Rouge: Louisiana State University, College of Education Administrative and Foundational Services; Walker, G., & Vilella-Velez, F. (1992). *Anatomy of a demonstration: STEP from pilot through replication and postprogram impacts.* Philadelphia: Public/Private Ventures.

56. Forum for Youth Investment. (2004).

57. Miller. (2003).

58. Canada, G. (2002, October). Improving outcomes for children and youth through a place-based strategy. Interview conducted by Mitch Nauffts at the *Philanthropy News Digest.* Available at http://fdncenter.org/pnd/newsmakers/nwsmkr.jhtml?id=15100011.

59. Wright. (2004).

60. Gambone, M. A., & Arbreton, A.J.A. (1997, April). *Safe havens: The contribution of youth organizations to healthy adolescent development.* Philadelphia: Public/Private Ventures.

61. Gambone & Arbreton. (1997).

SHERRI C. LAUVER *is a consultant at the Harvard Family Research Project. In July 2005, she will be assistant professor at the Warner Graduate School of Education at the University of Rochester, Rochester, New York.*

PRISCILLA M. D. LITTLE *is associate director of the Harvard Family Research Project and project manager of HFRP's Out-of-School Time Learning and Development Project.*

Methods for collecting attendance data in out-of-school-time programs depend on program goals, characteristics, and design.

5

Present and accounted for: Measuring attendance in out-of-school-time programs

Leila M. Fiester, Sandra D. Simpkins, Suzanne M. Bouffard

EVIDENCE THAT YOUTH PROGRAMS have real benefits has prompted efforts to get young people in the door of out-of-school-time (OST) programs.[1] Once youth are enrolled, attendance plays a key role in the participation equation. Children and youth will not benefit unless they attend programs regularly, and evidence is emerging that those who attend more frequently and for longer periods of time benefit more than their peers whose attendance is more sporadic.[2] As researchers and evaluators begin to tackle such questions as, "Why do youth benefit from programs?" and "How much does participation matter?" attendance data are the key to linking program participation with youth outcomes. Program leaders also need attendance data for program planning and to demonstrate to funders, government agencies, and other stakeholders that they are serving their targeted numbers and populations of youth well.

OST programs vary widely in the amount and frequency of services they offer, and young people vary in how often they take

NEW DIRECTIONS FOR YOUTH DEVELOPMENT, NO. 105, SPRING 2005 © WILEY PERIODICALS, INC.

advantage of these services. Some OST programs require daily attendance, while others operate on a voluntary drop-in basis. As a result, simply checking a box for "present" or "absent" does not provide enough information to link attendance to outcomes. Researchers and program personnel should also ask: How often do children attend, for how many hours per week, and for how many years? Techniques for measuring attendance and for answering these questions should be driven by the goals and needs of individual programs; there is no one method for measuring attendance that fulfills all purposes at all times.[3]

Why should programs measure attendance?

Attendance data in OST programs can be used for the following purposes:[4]

- *To gauge demand for services (in general and for specific activities).* Attendance data are a quick indicator of how attractive a program is to children and parents. If staff plan a special activity and attendance does not go up, chances are the activity did not work well. Directors also can use attendance data to identify services and staffing patterns that cause an increase or drop-off in participation. At many after-school programs, programming changes weekly. Directors can compare attendance rates on days when students work on academic activities with days when they take field trips to ascertain which schedule students prefer.
- *To support program-level planning and management.* Attendance data can help managers determine how many staff to hire, how much space to obtain, and how many supplies to order. The data also can reveal programming needs across age groups. For example, if the program serves grades K–8 but attendance data show that half the participants on a typical day are in grades 3 or 5, then it makes sense to concentrate resources on those grades.
- *To facilitate case management.* Some OST programs link participants with other services they may need, such as medical or

mental health assessment and care. For example, the after-school drop-in center operated by the P. F. Bresee Foundation in East Hollywood, Los Angeles, uses magnetically encoded swipe cards to track every activity a participant engages in each day. When administrators examine the attendance data, they also consider data on participants' school activities, hobbies, career goals, medical needs, and other factors. If a youth is not making progress, administrators can see whether factors other than inconsistent attendance are involved. Staff can then target interventions to specific youth.

• *To support student rewards, incentives, and sanctions.* Some OST programs offer financial incentives for participants or provide stipends for work performed in the program and in internships. Attendance data can track these activities for payment purposes. After School Matters, which operates after-school programs at thirty-five sites in Chicago, offers apprenticeship programs in the arts, technology, communication, and sports (for which students are paid a stipend) and drop-in clubs (which do not carry a stipend). Teachers at the sites enter attendance data into an on-line database, and school clerks use the information to generate students' paychecks.

• *For staff self-reflection, training, and education.* The After-School Corporation (TASC) sponsors 242 after-school projects, primarily in New York City, that serve students in grades K–12. Staff examine weekly attendance reports for each site to see if the site is achieving its standard. If it is not, program officers talk with the site coordinator about possible barriers and solutions. The administrator of TASC's database also uses attendance data to help site coordinators evaluate their programs. He may encourage a director to examine attendance by date, for example. If the site serves two hundred youth on Monday and Tuesday but by Friday has only one hundred participants, the director may decide to change the Friday activities.

• *To fulfill accountability requirements.* Program funders typically use attendance data to determine the daily cost per child, verify grantees' compliance with a targeted level of service (the utilization rate), and substantiate reimbursement claims made to city, state, or federal funding streams.

- *To advocate for more funding or for the use of specific strategies.* Baltimore's Safe and Sound Campaign, a citywide effort to improve the lives of infants, children, and youth, includes OST programs that serve about four thousand K–12 students every day. The campaign uses geocodes to array OST attendance data and program capacity by U.S. Census tract. After-school leaders can identify which neighborhoods have (and are filling) the most OST slots and which neighborhoods could benefit from more programs.
- *To monitor the quality and effectiveness of an overall initiative.* Data on OST participants' start and end dates and daily participation can reveal variations in attendance patterns over time. When combined with an internal performance monitoring system, these data suggest relationships between program implementation, attendance, and outcomes.
- *To evaluate participant outcomes.* Evaluations of OST programs and initiatives often compare attendance to data on student outcomes, such as academic achievement, prosocial behaviors, and emotional adjustment. These evaluations allow program staff and researchers to assess the effectiveness of the program in improving the lives of youth.

A program's method of measuring attendance depends on the purpose for collecting the data. For example, if the purpose is to support program planning and management, or leaders want to know whether their program is reaching the target population, they will have to measure attendance and demographic data of the individual children and youth attending the program. If the purpose is to gauge demand for services, a measure of the total number of youth attending will be important. If the purpose is to assess program quality and results, leaders need to know whether activities are appealing across grade levels and activities, whether the schedule serves families' needs, and whether the program has an impact on participants. To answer those questions, program staff or evaluators will need to collect attendance data by child, by grade level, and by activity.

Options for collecting attendance data fall on a continuum from minimal to extensive use of technology. In the traditional pen-and-paper approach, someone—usually an instructor, program assistant, or parent volunteer—makes a mark on a hard copy of the enrollment roster for every student who attends on a given day. Alternatively, students may sign in every time they attend, and the sign-in sheets are collected daily.

Programs that aggregate daily attendance data by the week, month, or year need to enter their data into a database in which numbers can be combined and manipulated. The simplest of these is housed on a personal computer. Several types of software are available to support databases.

Web-based systems offer more choices and flexibility in analyzing and reporting data. They are a growing trend in OST data tracking because they make program-level data available to a broad audience. The major systems marketed to OST programs (YouthServices.net, QSP, and KidTrax) customize the data elements, level of analysis, and reporting formats to the needs of each customer.

Programs that need detailed data with minimal burden on staff sometimes use swipe cards. Students receive ID cards with individual bar codes, which they present to electronic scanners as they enter and exit each day (or sometimes for each activity). The data are stored in Web-based systems or stand-alone PCs. This system requires the purchase of proprietary software and at least one scanner and computer per site, so it is the most resource-intensive option.

Four indicators of attendance: Absolute attendance, intensity, breadth, and duration

Just as OST programs have a variety of reasons for collecting attendance data, programs and researchers have several ways of measuring attendance. Through a comprehensive review of the literature on school- and community-based OST programs, Simpkins, Little, and Weiss have identified four separate indicators of attendance.[5]

Policymakers, program directors, funders, and other stakeholders are particularly interested in the use of attendance data to evaluate participant outcomes. The ultimate goal of OST programs is to promote positive outcomes for youth—socially, behaviorally, academically, and in other ways—and a substantial body of research demonstrates that OST programs do benefit young people.[6] However, key questions remain. How often must participants attend in order to benefit? Does participating in multiple activities produce greater benefits than focusing on one activity? In order to answer questions such as these, researchers and program personnel must clearly understand and measure program attendance. However, most research has relied on a simple yes-or-no classification system for attendance, which has limited the ability of the field to answer these important questions.

Simpkins, Little, and Weiss identified over eighty research and evaluation studies that linked OST attendance with youth outcomes and included quantitative results with tests of statistical significance.[7] These studies included four indicators of attendance: an absolute indicator of attendance, intensity of attendance, duration of attendance, and breadth of attendance. Most research has relied on absolute attendance, the most basic indicator, and the fields of both practice and research are ripe for more detailed measures of attendance.

Absolute attendance

Most studies that have measured attendance in youth programs have used a yes or no indicator of absolute attendance. This general measure provides a minimal amount of information: whether a young person attended a program at all, regardless of the number of days or weeks. Absolute attendance is the most common indicator of attendance in OST programs. Among the eighty-three studies reviewed, fifty-six collected only absolute attendance data, and only twenty-seven used a more detailed measure of attendance. A likely explanation for this finding is that absolute attendance is often the easiest, fastest, and most cost-effective indicator to measure.

The level of information provided by absolute attendance is useful for some purposes. For example, local and national organizations and government agencies publish statistics on the number and percentage of youth attending OST programs to make a case for investments in the OST field. Their goal is to present the forest rather than the trees, that is, to provide a broad picture rather than a highly detailed one. However, absolute attendance excludes the information needed for program planning, accountability requirements, and assessment of youth outcomes.

Intensity

Attendance intensity is defined as the amount of time youth participate in an OST program in a given period of time. Intensity is also referred to as dosage, drawing on medical terminology for the amount of exposure to a treatment. Intensity can be measured on several time scales—hours per day, days per week, sessions per month, percentage of days the program was offered, and others—depending on how the program is designed. For instance, if activities change every few hours during the day and program leaders want to know whether students who attend for two hours every day have different outcomes from those who attend for half an hour per day, the program will need data in hours per day.

Simpkins, Little, and Weiss found that evaluators and researchers measured intensity in three ways depending on the goals of the evaluation and the program:[8]

Hours per day or per week. Petit, Laird, Bates, and Dodge classified intensity of participation by creating a variable for high, medium, and low participation, where high participators attended for four or more hours per week, medium participators attended for one to three hours per week, and low participators did not attend for any hours.[9]

Days or sessions per week. Some programs measure intensity by the number of days per session or per week that youth attend. For example, evaluators of programs sponsored by TASC classified youth as active participators if they attended the program for three or more days per week, as nonactive participators if they attended for fewer than three days per week, and as nonparticipators if they did not attend at all.[10] Another approach, which was taken by evaluators of the Boys & Girls Clubs, is to divide the group of program participants into three categories according to who attended most and least often in order to create groups of high, moderate, and low attenders.[11]

Days or sessions in the past year. Some programs have used the number of sessions in the past year to define participators and nonparticipators (for example, ten or more sessions versus fewer than ten sessions)[12] or to categorize high and low participators (thirty-five or more days per year versus less than thirty-five days).[13] One evaluation of programs in central Ohio classified high and moderate participators based on the percentage of available program days in which youth participated (79 percent or more the days the program was offered versus less than 79 percent of the days).[14]

Intensity data serve several functions. They can inform programs about patterns of participation among individual families and groups of families. For example, if children attend the program an average of one day per week, families probably are not using the program as their primary means of OST supervision. Intensity data can also help determine how much participation matters. Research generally shows that young people who attend with high levels of intensity have more positive academic, social, and behavioral outcomes than youth with low intensity. In the academic realm, students who participate with more intensity demonstrate higher grades and test scores, more homework completion, more positive attitudes toward school, and higher rates of high school completion than their peers.[15] In the social and behavioral realms, those who participate with high levels of intensity engage in more community service, less problematic behavior, and less substance use, and they report more optimistic views of the future and better emotional adjustment.[16] Although most research indicates that high intensity is preferable, some research suggests that a moderate level of intensity is best. This finding may suggest that adolescents who are heavily involved in one extracurricular activity (for example, a sports team) are constrained from pursuing other beneficial activities. It also highlights the insight that can be gained from collecting intensity data.

Duration

Attendance duration refers to the length of participation over time, usually measured in number of years. For example, one youth's attendance may have a duration of one year, while another youth's attendance may have a duration of two years, even though they both attended the same program with the same intensity of three days per week. Duration may also be measured in number of weeks, number of terms, or number of program sessions, depending on the needs and design of specific programs. Data on attendance duration show whether children are in the same program year after year. They can inform program stakeholders about the OST needs of the community, and they can help program staff and evaluators assess whether youth who participate for longer periods of time benefit more than their peers who participate for shorter periods of time.

Of the studies Simpkins, Little, and Weiss reviewed, relatively few measured attendance duration. Those studies that did found longer attendance duration to be associated with more positive youth outcomes.[17] For example, an evaluation of a 4-H program found that youth who attended the program for at least one year engaged in less delinquent and substance abuse behavior and had more positive attitudes and relationships with adults than youth who attended for shorter periods of time.[18] In another 4-H study, those who participated for more than a year had more positive outcomes than those who participated for less than a year in the areas of communication, conflict resolution, grades, homework, and volunteering.[19] Children who participated for less than a year benefited more than those who had not participated at all.

In the studies described, greater attendance duration of any length was related to increasingly large benefits for youth. In other cases, however, there may be a minimum threshold for duration; that is, participants must attend for a certain amount of time in order to benefit. For example, studies of programs supported by TASC (New

York) and Los Angeles's Better Educated Students for Tomorrow found that participants had higher academic achievement than non-participants, but only after participating for two years.[20]

Breadth

Program staff and researchers know that young people have many choices for OST activities, and many participate in multiple programs and activities.[21] Breadth of attendance refers to the range of programs and activities in which youth participate. Some youth achieve breadth by attending several programs during the week, while others participate in one program that includes a combination of activities.

Although many programs offer breadth in activities, few evaluations measure this information or attempt to tie it to youth outcomes. Most studies focus on youth attendance in one program and do not include information on the specific activities experienced within programs. Even when researchers use an experimental evaluation design to assign youth to a program or control group, the control group's attendance in other OST programs or their participation in multiple activities within the program often is ignored. One reason may be the difficulty of gathering reliable data on which activities youth participate in within a program (although computerized attendance tracking systems are making this more feasible). Similarly, evaluators may find it cumbersome or even intrusive to ask participants about their other OST pursuits outside the program.

Although breadth of attendance is the hardest indicator to assess and the least researched, it can yield valuable information and results for youth programs. Programs may need breadth in order to achieve intensity and duration.[22] In other words, providing a range of interesting activities may be necessary to retain participants' interest and attendance. The limited research that has been conducted so far also suggests that breadth is associated with more positive youth outcomes. One study of a multicomponent OST program in Texas examined how many activities youth participated in within the program; elementary school children who participated in three or more activities received higher grades and test scores than those who participated in one or two activities.[23] This finding is particularly striking because the study found no difference in some of the outcomes on the basis of absolute participation. The results therefore suggest that breadth offers important information above and beyond other indicators of attendance, but more research is needed to determine whether breadth is in fact related to more positive youth outcomes.

Combining indicators

Attendance intensity, duration, and breadth can be combined for a rich portrait of youth participation in OST programs. For instance, the indicators collectively can answer questions about the benefits of attending every day for a short period of time versus attending sporadically over a longer period of time. Few studies to date have combined the indicators, but those that have show the value of this approach.

An evaluation of TASC projects combined intensity and duration.[24] Youth who were highly active (or had high levels of attendance intensity) for two years had the highest increases in math test scores and school attendance. Scores on these outcomes were higher than those of youth who were active for two years, which were in turn higher than those of youth who were active for only one year. Nonactive participants (those who attended on an irregular basis) did not demonstrate any academic gains. Similarly, an evaluation of the SFBI, which runs OST youth and family centers at public schools in low-income neighborhoods, combined duration and breadth, examining attendance in terms of the number of sessions (fall, spring, and summer) and the number of activities (educational activities only or educational plus other activities).[25] Youth who attended the program during all three sessions and participated in educational and other activities experienced increases in leadership behavior, school effort, and feelings of self-efficacy. In contrast, participants with the same duration (three sessions) but less breadth (educational activities only) experienced increases only in school effort.

Which attendance data should programs collect?

With multiple reasons for collecting attendance data and many options for measuring the data, which attendance indicators should programs collect? In an ideal world, programs would collect data on all four indicators of attendance. That expectation is unrealistic for many programs, however, due to the time and cost burdens. Most programs have to choose just a few types of data to collect, and the right approach depends on the goals of the program.

If the program aims to build skills (such as academic and cognitive skills), knowing the intensity of participation might be most important.[26] If the program aims to foster social competence, knowing the duration of each participant's engagement might be most important. If program staff want to know whether competing activities prevent some youth from attending regularly, collecting information on the breadth of activities attended outside the program will be important.

Program design also influences the choice of indicators. If a youth is allowed to attend for only one year, for instance, then duration is not an important indicator.

Once the indicators of attendance have been chosen, there are practical factors to consider:

• Complex data systems are harder to feed and maintain than simple ones, so it is best to keep data collection as simple as possible. Researchers and program directors suggest that the following data elements represent a good minimum standard: site name (if part of a multisite initiative or citywide database); total number of students enrolled; total head count per day, week, and month; student names; individualized student number (such as a school- or district-assigned identification code); age or grade in school (or both); each student's first and last date of enrollment; and each student's demographic information (for example, gender, ethnicity, neighborhood).

• Is the program open every day? Attendance data usually are collected daily (or on every day the program is offered). Daily attendance can be aggregated to obtain the monthly attendance rate, but the reverse is not possible.

• How large is the program (that is, how many children need to be tracked)? A small number can be tracked using pen-and-paper methods, but a large number may require electronic capacity.

• If the program is school based, do students leave the building between the regular and after-school day? If so, the after-school program cannot necessarily rely on data collected by the school program (for example, through the school system's scanners and swipe cards) and will have to reenter its own data.

• Do all students participate in the same activity at the same time, or do groups of students rotate through activities? If everyone does the same thing at the same time, it may be possible to gauge the effects of participation by collecting data on which students walked in the door at the beginning of each day.

• Do some activities occur offsite? If so, a centralized sign-in location at the main program site will not be sufficient to capture data on all students.

• How much money and staff time are available for data tracking, and how important is it for the program to invest resources in the activity? (Invest too little in data collection, and the effort will not produce the information needed for accountability reports or program improvement. Invest too much, and scarce resources may be wasted.)

• What is the age of the young people served by the program? Age is a key consideration in determining optimal patterns of attendance and methods of data collection. For example, it is reasonable to expect elementary school–age children to participate in programs with an intensity of four to five days a week, but the reality for middle and high school students is quite different. Competing demands of work, play, and the desire to hang out with friends render five-days-a-week attendance expectations unrealistic. Many programs for middle and high school youth set their thresholds for maximum participation at three days per week, in recognition of these competing demands.

Because the needs and goals of OST programs are diverse, there is no one right approach to collecting attendance data. For example, considerations such as cost, personnel, and data analysis will vary according to the needs and resources of individual programs. These logistical considerations play an important role in the processes of getting and using attendance data. Similarly, there is no one right indicator of attendance. However, it is clear that measuring attendance in absolute terms—that is, participation versus nonparticipation—is not sufficient. This measure does not provide enough information for linking participation to outcomes, for programs' self-reflection and improvement, or for meeting the accountability requirements that are increasingly a reality for OST programs. Appropriate measurement of attendance is the cornerstone of a thoughtful evaluation to demonstrate effectiveness and inform program improvement. Engaging in a process of self-reflection about individual needs and goals can help programs to decide why and how to collect attendance data and to understand how these data will play a role in improving the program and the lives of youth.

Notes

1. See Chapter Four, this volume.

2. Simpkins, S. C., Little, P. M. D., & Weiss, H. B. (2004). *Understanding and measuring attendance in out-of-school time programs*. Cambridge, MA: Harvard Family Research Project.

3. Some of the material presented in this chapter is excerpted from the following two reports: Fiester, L., with Policy Studies Associates. (2004). *After-school counts! A guide to issues and strategies for monitoring attendance in afterschool and other youth programs*. New York: After School Project, Robert Wood Johnson Foundation. Simpkins et al. (2004).

4. Fiester, with Policy Studies Associates. (2004).

5. Simpkins et al. (2004).

6. Eccles, J. S., & Gootman, J. A. (Eds.). (2002). *Community programs to promote youth development*. Washington, DC: National Academy Press; Gambone, M. A., Klem, A. M., & Connell, J. P. (2002). *Finding out what matters for youth: Testing key links in a community action framework for youth development*. Philadelphia: Youth Development Strategies and Institute for Research and Reform in Education; Little, P. M. D., & Harris, E. (2003). *A review of out-of-school time program quasi-experimental and experimental evaluation results*. Cambridge, MA: Harvard Family Research Project. Available at www.gse.harvard.

edu/hfrp/projects/afterschool/resources/snapshot1.html; Mahoney, J. L., & Cairns, R. B. (1997). Do extracurricular activities protect against early school dropout? *Developmental Psychology, 33*(2), 241–253; Posner, J. K., & Vandell, D. L. (1994). Low-income children's after-school care: Are there beneficial effects of after-school programs? *Child Development, 65,* 440–456; Simpkins, S. (2003). Does youth participation in out-of-school time activities make a difference? *Evaluation Exchange, 9*(1). Available at www.gse.harvard.edu/hfrp/eval/issue21/theory.html.

    7. Simpkins et al. (2004).

    8. Simpkins et al. (2004).

    9. Pettit, G. S., Laird, R. D., Bates, J. E., & Dodge, K. A. (1997). Patterns of after-school care in middle childhood: Risk factors and development outcomes. *Merrill-Palmer Quarterly, 43,* 515–538.

    10. White, R. N., Reisner, E. R., Welsh, M., & Russell, C. (2001). *Patterns of student-level change linked to TASC participation: Based on TASC projects in year 2.* Washington, DC: Policy Studies Associates.

    11. Anderson-Butcher, D., Newsome, W. S., & Ferrari, T. M. (2003). Participation in Boys and Girls Clubs and relationships to youth outcomes. *Journal of Community Psychology, 31*(1), 39–55.

    12. Mayer, R. E., Quilici, J., Moreno, R., Duran, R., Woodbridge, S., Simon, R., Sanchez, D., & Lavezzo, A. (1997). Cognitive consequences of participation in a fifth dimension after-school computer club. *Journal of Educational Computing Research, 16,* 353–369.

    13. University of California at Irvine, Department of Education. (2002). *Evaluation of California's AfterSchool Learning and Safe Neighborhoods Partnerships Program: 1999–2001.* Irvine, CA: Author.

    14. Anderson-Butcher, D. (2002). *Youth development programs in central Ohio: An evaluation report for the City of Columbus and United Way of Central Ohio.* Columbus: Center for Learning Excellence, Ohio State University.

    15. Anderson-Butcher et al. (2003); Brown, R., & Evans, W. P. (2002). Extracurricular activity and ethnicity: Creating greater school connection among diverse student populations. *Urban Education, 37*(1), 41–58; Cooper, H., Valentine, J. C., Nye, B., & Lindsay, J. L. (1999). Relationships between five after-school activities and academic achievement. *Journal of Educational Psychology, 91,* 369–378; Grossman, J. B., Resch, N. L., & Tierney, J. P. (2000). *Making a difference: An impact study of Big Brothers, Big Sisters.* Philadelphia: Public/Private Ventures; Marsh, H. W., & Kleitman, S. (2002). Extracurricular school activities: The good, the bad, and the nonlinear. *Educational Review, 72,* 464–514; Mayer et al. (1997); Posner, J. K., & Vandell, D. L. (1999). After-school activities and the development of low-income urban children: A longitudinal study. *Developmental Psychology, 35,* 868–879; Schinke, S. P., Cole, K. C., & Poulin, S. R. (2000). Enhancing the educational achievement of at-risk youth. *Prevention Science, 1,* 51–60; U.S. Department of Education, Office of the Under Secretary. (2003). *When schools stay open late: The national evaluation of the 21st Century Community Learning Centers program, first year findings.* Washington, DC: Author; White et al. (2001).

16. Anderson-Butcher et al. (2003); Grossman, J. B., Price, M. L., Fellerath, V., Jucovy, L. Z., Kotloff, L. J., Raley, R., & Walker, K. (2002). *Multiple choices after school: Findings from the Extended-Service Schools Initiative.* Philadelphia: Public/Private Ventures. Available at www.mdrc.org/publications/48/full.pdf; Jordan, W. J., & Nettles, S. M. (2000). How students invest their time outside of school: Effects on school-related outcomes. *Social Psychology of Education, 3*(4), 217–243; Marsh & Kleitman. (2002); Mazza, J. J., & Eggert, L. L. (2001). Activity involvement among suicidal and nonsuicidal high-risk and typical adolescents. *Suicide and Life-Threatening Behavior, 31,* 265–281; Posner & Vandell. (1999); University of California at Irvine, Department of Education. (2002); Youniss, J., McLellan, J. A., Su, Y., & Yates, M. (1999). The role of community service in identity development: Normative, unconventional, and deviant orientations. *Journal of Adolescent Research, 14*(2), 248–261.

17. Simpkins et al. (2004).

18. Astroth, K. A., & Haynes, G. W. (2002). More than cows and cooking: Newest research shows the impact of 4-H. *Journal of Extension, 40*(4). Available at www.joe.org/joe/2002august/a6.shtml.

19. Rodriguez, E., Hirschl, T. A., Mead, J. P., & Groggin, S. E. (1999). *Understanding the difference 4-H Clubs make in the lives of New York youth: How 4-H contributes to positive youth development.* Ithaca, NY: Cornell University.

20. Brooks, P. E., Mojica, C. M., & Land, R. E. (1995). *Final evaluation report: Longitudinal study of LA's BEST after school education and enrichment program, 1992–94.* Los Angeles: Center for the Study of Evaluation, Graduate School of Education & Information Studies, University of California; Welsh, M. E., Russell, C. A., Williams, I., Reisner, E. R., & White, R. N. (2002). *Promoting learning and school attendance through after-school programs: Student-level changes in educational performance across TASC's first three years.* Washington, DC: Policy Studies Associates. Available at http://www.tascorp.org/programs/research/S34_student_level_change.pdf.

21. Larson, R. W. (2001). How U.S. children and adolescents spend time: What it does (and doesn't) tell us about their development. *Current Directions in Psychological Science, 10*(5), 160–164.

22. Walker, K. (2004, July 9). *Understanding participation in out-of-school time programs (commentary).* Paper presented at Getting and Using Data to Improve Out-of-School Time Programs: Exploring Key Participation Issues, Cambridge, MA.

23. Baker, D., & Witt, P. A. (1996). Evaluation of the impact of two after-school recreation programs. *Journal of Park and Recreation Administration, 14*(3), 60–81.

24. Welsh et al. (2002).

25. Walker, K. E., & Arbreton, A. J. A. (2004). *After-school pursuits: An examination of outcomes in the San Francisco Beacon Initiative.* Philadelphia: Public/Private Ventures.

26. Walker, K. (2004).

LEILA M. FIESTER *is an independent consultant. She prepared portions of the work presented here with Policy Studies Associates for Afterschool Counts! published by the Robert Wood Johnson Foundation.*

SANDRA D. SIMPKINS *is an assistant professor in the Department of Family and Human Development at Arizona State University and was a research associate at the Harvard Family Research Project.*

SUZANNE M. BOUFFARD *is a research analyst at the Harvard Family Research Project and a doctoral candidate in developmental psychology at Duke University in Durham, North Carolina.*

How do out-of-school-time programs get from attendance to active engagement? School researchers propose that engagement is composed of three "ABC" components, affect, behavior, and cognition, which can also be applied to out-of-school-time programs.

6

The ABCs of engagement in out-of-school-time programs

W. Todd Bartko

IT IS NOT SURPRISING that research on schooling and children's academic experiences could occupy a large library. All children in the United States are mandated to attend school, and improving teaching and learning are longstanding national priorities. Yet the choices that children, adolescents, and parents make about how youth spend their out-of-school time (OST) are critical for their current and future well-being. It is only recently, however, that researchers have become interested in studying the OST experiences of children and youth. This newly found interest began in the mid-1990s, coinciding with the beginning of direct federal funding of after-school programs.

Research on after-school programs grew rapidly following the Clinton administration's investment in after-school programs, initially conceived as a vehicle for curbing youth crime. It is now well known that the after-school hours from 3:00 P.M. to 6:00 P.M. are the peak time for crimes committed by juveniles and for engaging

NEW DIRECTIONS FOR YOUTH DEVELOPMENT, NO. 105, SPRING 2005 © WILEY PERIODICALS, INC.

in drug, alcohol, and cigarette use and sexual activities. Not surprisingly, this is the period of the day when many children and teens are on their own due to parents' work demands. Furthermore, the increase in the number of dual-earner families and the welfare-to-work policies that took many single mothers out of the home and placed them back in the workforce created public demand for more adult-supervised activities after school. The Clinton administration, with wide bipartisan support in Congress, expanded the original Jeffords-Gunderson legislation from an initial $25 million in 1994 to $800 million in 1999, marking the most rapid increase in funding for any federal program in history.

As a result of the tremendous commitment by the federal government and the increased demand for services, after-school opportunities expanded rapidly—and perhaps too rapidly. Some of these programs seemed to be built on the notion that "if you build it, they will come."[1] Without sufficient grounding in the developmental needs of children and youth and without adequate outreach to families, attracting and sustaining involvement was problematic. Often youth attended these programs only intermittently, and program staff worked frantically to design activities that captured the interests of their young participants.

In addition, within a few years of the dramatic increase in funding for after-school programs, stipulations for grantees were added that mandated a focus on academic achievement in addition to the recreational, health, and social service activities. Some youth regarded this as an extension of the school day rather than as an opportunity to participate in fun activities after school. As a result, the challenge to encourage and sustain participation over the long term remains.

Not surprisingly, the pace with which programs have evolved has left researchers playing catch-up, not an unfamiliar role. There is mounting evidence, however, that youth participation in structured, skill-based activities is linked to improved academic performance, positive physical and mental health, lower rates of substance abuse, and rewarding social relationships.[2] There is also some indication that experiences in safe, supportive, and growth-enhancing environments may be especially important for at-risk youth, particularly those from troubled families.³ This body of literature, however, is far from complete and suffers from many of the same growing pains confronting OST programs.

Engagement as the missing link

The central question for this chapter and for both research and practice in the OST arena is, "Given the link between participation and healthy outcomes, how do we get from participation to sustained engagement?" In the Weiss, Little, and Bouffard model of participation set out in Chapter One of this issue, sustained engagement in an activity or multiple activities is posited to lead to more positive outcomes than casual or irregular participation. Both research and common sense tell us that youth who are committed to and highly active in an endeavor are more likely to continue in that endeavor, see it as part of their identity, and benefit from successful participation.

Research conducted in this area by my colleagues and me attempts to understand the factors related to engagement in activities using a model of engagement developed to better understand children's school experiences. In this model, we reasoned that the more children feel connected to their schools as institutions of learning, the more likely they will be to do what is expected of them, try hard, and persevere.⁴ Our notions of school engagement are drawn from several related literatures, including research on motivation, self-regulated learning, and school climate. These literatures, however, are largely disjointed. One of the goals of our school engagement work was to better integrate previous research into a model that captures the dynamics of children's behaviors, thoughts, and emotions.

Indeed, our work has capitalized on engagement as a multidimensional construct that encompasses each of the three components. This conceptualization of engagement as an interplay of affect, behavior, and cognition can provide a richer characterization of children at school than any of the research on single components.

In reality, the three components are dynamically embedded within a single individual and are not isolated processes.

The ABCs of engagement

Engagement is best represented by three interrelated components: affect, behavior, and cognition—the ABC model. Affective engagement refers to positive and negative reactions to teachers, classmates, the academic curriculum, or school. It also is defined as having feelings of belonging and of valuing learning and the broader goals of schooling. Behavioral engagement is related to participation; it includes involvement in academic and social activities in the classroom, including conduct, attention, following rules, and effort. Cognitive engagement refers to investment in learning; it includes being thoughtful and willing to exert the effort necessary to comprehend complex ideas and master difficult skills.

It is helpful to think about the three components of engagement as a triad rather than individually since none occurs in a vacuum. Some of our previous research on school engagement shows that for some students, affect, behavior, and cognition follow the same patterns (for example, all high or all low). For others, the components appear to be unlinked. To take one example, some students reported high cognitive and behavioral engagement but low affective engagement. These students followed the rules and did the work but were not necessarily committed to learning or did not feel a connection to their teachers or classmates. These findings show the importance of looking at the three components simultaneously rather than individually, as is frequently done in educational studies.

In OST settings, similar patterns may be common, with some youth viewing the activities as a way to fill time after school rather than as an important opportunity to learn valued skills. Conversely, program staff will be familiar with the description of young people who attend programs to be with friends and therefore may be highly affectively engaged but are otherwise not highly behaviorally or cognitively motivated.

With regard to OST, the three components of engagement seem equally applicable and perhaps even more so. Many OST programs work to foster a sense of belonging among participating youth, as well as warm and supporting interpersonal relationships among participants and staff. Similarly, participation in OST activities implies behavioral engagement to some extent. However, high behavioral engagement refers not just to participation but to a high degree of effort. Finally, cognitive engagement in activities refers to a willingness on the part of youth to invest time and effort in learning the skills necessary for the activity. Given that OST programs are not constrained by a state-mandated curriculum as are most schools and classrooms, programs can be designed and run in ways that truly capture the interests, talents, and imaginations of young people and in effect elicit engagement.

Early precursors of engagement in OST

As part of our previous work on school engagement, we interviewed a number of young children about their involvement in OST programs. This was a preliminary effort at assessing the fit of the engagement model to this area of research. Within the sample of third and fifth graders from three inner-city areas in the Midwest, we found few students participating in OST programs. The majority of these children spent their after-school hours at home, at a relative's home, or in unsupervised settings in their neighborhoods. Therefore, it was not possible to get a clear picture of what engagement in activities might look like for these young children. Furthermore, because participation was largely infrequent, we were not able to follow children's activity participation over time to better understand the factors related to sustained engagement.

However, for the children who were involved in OST programs, their comments give us an early view of the situational and interpersonal resources that capture their interests, and these are in line with the affective, behavioral, and cognitive components of engagement. For example, the importance of having time to interact with peers and of participating in project-based learning is evident in this response from a fifth-grade girl:

I used to [be in an after-school program], but it is over now. It was called the Discovery Program. It was every Saturday in the morning. It was sort of like school, but no one got homework. We learn about things like hurricanes and volcanoes, do projects there, and lots of fun things. It was really nice, the people were nice. You got to meet new people, and you learn new things. They said that maybe I could be like a volunteer [next year] and help the kids.

This is a good example of a positive affective experience through meeting and connecting with new people and intellectual appeal in the curriculum of the program, as well as the future opportunity for leadership. Although this program ended, it is clear that this student would have chosen to continue to participate, given the chance. The importance of leadership for children's involvement is a crucial piece of the engagement process.

The appeal of spending time with peers is also seen in this comment from a ten-year-old boy, who is not drawn by the activities offered in his current after-school program and who would prefer to attend the YWCA: "I'd like to go to the YMCA 'cause a lot of my friends go there, and I'd get to go have fun with all my friends when we're not in school, 'cause we'd have more time to talk."

Engagement in appealing tasks or novel learning environments that differ from typical classroom assignments is another way to sustain interest in a program. One young boy told us about using computers in his after-school program:

Go on the computer, I like computers a lot. We use them to go on the Internet, find out what there is on the Net. Also I like to explore around, like go on vacation to Europe and the Bahamas and those places. It's kind of cool, 'cause you don't have to explore too much to find out things, and the computer also gives you information about like the Eiffel Tower and also what I like about the computer is that there's nice things to do on it. You could make like a letter and print it out.

Programs aimed at fostering children's existing interests and abilities within an empowering and supportive environment would clearly be more likely to lead to both cognitive and affective engagement. One young girl described how her interest in performing arts is enhanced in the program she attends:

I'm in soccer, chess, and Growing Up/Speaking Out for girls. We're having a play. It's a poem class. And you're gonna see me two times solo, 'cause we each get to do our own thing two times, and the rest is like group. And we have this one thing, it's like a bird, we're all like little birds and we fly in and we fly out.

These examples give some indications of how early experiences in programs can sustain or inhibit subsequent participation. In the future, we hope to be able to talk with adolescents who have been active in one or more OST areas or activities to learn how well the engagement model captures their affective, behavioral, and cognitive experiences over time.

What do practitioners need to do to foster engagement?

Getting children and teens from participation to engagement in an activity or program does not simply require more of the same. Rather, program staff need to be attuned to the affective, behavioral, and cognitive demands of the activity within the context of the developmental needs of and resources available to participants. This is no small task, especially for programs with limited financial resources, staffed by individuals without significant background or training in these issues, with little support and involvement from families, and yet high expectations from the community.

What types of contexts may foster engagement? The youth development literature details aspects of contexts that are related to positive development and growth experiences. There is mounting evidence that children's everyday experiences and the contexts in which those experiences occur tell us a great deal about both children's current well-being and future life chances. Children do better across a range of developmental outcomes when their daily settings:

- Are safe and free of dangers
- Have clear and consistent rules that are enforced
- Are warm and supportive with opportunities to connect to others
- Present opportunities for inclusion and belonging
- Have clear social norms concerning behavior
- Are governed by practices that support both autonomy and responsibility
- Provide opportunities to learn valued skills
- Are connected with each other and consistent in the expectations, values, and practices communicated to the child[5]

These aspects of positive developmental contexts apply equally well to in-school and out-of-school settings. For instance, there is broad evidence that warm and supportive yet structured school classrooms with high expectations on the part of teachers are associated with high motivation and academic achievement.[6] It seems logical that out-of-school settings that support and encourage youth while providing challenging and stimulating activities would be most likely to lead to engagement and, subsequently, to positive psychological, social, and academic functioning.

How do we work to create these types of OST contexts and get children and youth involved?

- *Practitioners must get children in the door.* Outreach to youth and their parents is crucial, either directly through telephone calls, home visits, or presentations at schools, or indirectly through word of mouth. The first few visits to a program are critical since youth (like all of us) quickly develop initial impressions of the activity setting and how well it fits their needs and interests, the competence and personal qualities of the staff, and the degree of comfort and familiarity of peers.
- *Safety is a primary concern of many participants and their parents.* This issue was mentioned frequently in our school engagement interviews with children attending urban schools. Many of them were very concerned about safety issues in the neighborhoods around the schools and also talked repeatedly about fighting among

students. They sometimes described it as horseplay that escalated out of control. Safety is clearly one of the core aspects of contexts that foster positive youth development. Yet we often think only of the physical safety of children and much less about the psychological bullying and interpersonal conflicts that can occur in any setting.

• *Engagement in activities and programs is more likely to occur when youth have opportunities for stimulating and challenging experiences.* Although there is some need for down time, particularly in the after-school hours, young people want the time, resources, and instruction to help them improve at skill-based activities ranging from sports to academics to performing arts. This refers mostly to cognitive engagement, learning skills to master a desired task, but the excitement that often accompanies the mastery process also relates to the affective component of engagement.

• *Program leaders must be competent, knowledgeable, and accepting, together with firm behavioral control and high expectations for participants.* Affective engagement, or the feeling of belonging combined with positive views of adults and peers, is a critical component to sustained involvement. Some youth may tolerate activity settings that are not interpersonally comfortable if they perceive a large payoff in terms of skill development, but a warm and supportive atmosphere is certainly desirable for most of us and a necessary condition for some. It is also important to note that optimal environments for children are warm and supportive as well as challenging. Research on school interventions suggests that improving the climate of schools is not itself sufficient to improve learning.[7] Teachers must also have clear expectations for their students regarding classroom behavior, completing homework, working with others, and performing to the best of one's abilities. In short, youth are more likely to be engaged in an activity where they feel comfortable, accepted, and challenged.

• *Programs need to both foster and take advantage of the relationships among participants.* Many youth choose to attend programs because they have a close friend who attends. Yet engagement in a particular activity or project is more likely to result when youth feel as if they are part of a group. This is best illustrated by the fascinating work by Milbrey McLaughlin who encourages teens to take on leadership roles in OST settings—in effect, to develop their own programs while working together as a team.[8] This work is striking because it reframes the view that many adults have of adolescent peer groups as the root cause of deviant behavior by showing that teens are willing and able to take on the responsibility for structuring their own time in ways that are constructive, rewarding, and beneficial for the community.

Future research

There is a converging body of research on the characteristics of family, school, peer, neighborhood, and other contexts that are likely to promote the healthy development of children and adolescents. Safe, warm, supportive, and challenging environments allow youth to identify and develop their interests and abilities, connect with peers and adults, and avoid unhealthy and dangerous behaviors. These types of environments, while beneficial for all young people, are critically important for children and teens at risk for school failure or problem behavior or for youth from disruptive or neglectful family circumstances. To the extent that both school and out-of-school activity settings can provide these supportive contexts, youth are much more likely to finish school, develop strong relationships with others, and feel good about who they are and their future life chances.

In OST, much research is still needed. For example, we know very little about how much youth need to participate in OST programs to reap the benefits, that is, whether there is a "dose-response" effect. We do not yet have good data on which children and youth benefit the most from participation. Finely grained studies that detail what specific activities are linked to positive outcomes or the dynamics of social relationships that occur within these programs have not yet been done. In short, there is much to be done before we have a clear picture linking participation to healthy development.

We also know very little about how best to balance children's school and activity participation and leisure time. Much of the research on OST has taken a piecemeal approach, examining the links between participation in one or two activity settings and psychosocial functioning. Given the constraints on how youth spend their time, however, it is important to better understand where participation in programs fits into the daily lives of young people. In a previous study, my colleagues and I found several different patterns of time use among a large sample of twelfth graders.[9] Patterns included youth who were highly active in several extracurricular areas, youth who were primarily involved in sports, students who reported being highly involved in school activities, and largely uninvolved youth. These patterns were linked to academic, psychological, and social outcomes in different ways, suggesting that activity participation needs to be examined within the larger view of family, school, and peer contexts. This may be especially true for at-risk youth living in less-than-optimal family situations or children attending poorly performing schools.

There is also little research devoted to factors that help youth to sustain their participation in activity settings. We have presented some very preliminary work based on a model of engagement developed around children's school experiences. Much more research in this area is needed. In particular, we need to know more about the activities themselves that occur at after-school programs; that is, what activities appeal to what children under what circumstances? Which children benefit the most from participation in these programs? How can programs be made more accessible? Most important, we need good longitudinal research on children's sustained participation over time.

This chapter has put forth some ideas about how to foster engagement with attention to the affective, behavioral, and cognitive aspects of settings. These ideas, drawn from work on educational and workplace settings, seem equally applicable to OST programs. Further data will help to test this hypothesis and narrow the focus on the most critical features of OST programs for both sustaining engagement and nurturing healthy development.

120   PARTICIPATION IN YOUTH PROGRAMS

Notes

1. Gordon, C., & Gordon, L. (producers), and Robinson, P. A. (director). (1997). *Field of dreams* [motion picture]. Universal Studios.

2. Eccles, J. S., & Barber, B. (in press). Adolescents' activity involvement: Predictors and longitudinal consequences. *Journal of Adolescent Research*; Larson, R., & Kleiber, D. (1993). Free time activities as factors in adolescent adjustment. In P. Tolan & B. Cohler (Eds.), *Handbook of clinical research and practice with adolescents* (pp. 125–145). New York: Wiley; Mahoney, J. L., & Cairns, R. B. (1997). Do extracurricular activities protect against early school dropout? *Developmental Psychology, 33*, 241–253; Marsh, H. (1992). Extracurricular activities: Beneficial extension of the traditional curriculum or subversion of academic goals? *Journal of Educational Psychology, 84*(4), 553–562; Marsh, H., & Kleitman, S. (2002). Extracurricular school activities: The good, the bad, and the nonlinear. *Harvard Educational Review, 72*(4), 464–511; McNeal, R. (1995). Extracurricular activities and high school dropouts. *Sociology of Education, 68*, 62–81; Youniss, J., Yates, M., & Su, Y. (1997). Social integration: Community service and marijuana use in high school seniors. *Journal of Adolescent Research, 12*, 245–262.

3. Mahoney, J. (2000). School extracurricular activity participation as a moderator in the development of antisocial patterns. *Child Development, 71*, 502–516.

4. Blumenfeld, P., Modell, J., Bartko, T., Secada, W., Fredricks, J., Friedel, J., & Paris, A. (in press). School engagement of inner city students during middle childhood. In C. Cooper, C. Garcia Coll, T. Bartko, C. Chatman, & H. Davis (Eds.), *Developmental pathways through middle childhood: Rethinking contexts and diversity as resources.* Mahwah, NJ: Erlbaum.

5. Eccles, J. & Gootman, J. (Eds.). (2002). *Community programs to promote youth development.* National Research Council and Institute of Medicine, Board on Children, Youth, and Families, Committee on Community-Level Programs for Youth. Washington, DC: National Academy Press.

6. Wentzel, K. (1997). Student motivation in middle school: The role of perceived pedagogical caring. *Journal of Educational Psychology, 90*, 202–209; Skinner, E., & Belmont, M. J. (1993). Motivation in the classroom: Reciprocal effect of teacher behavior and student engagement across the school year. *Journal of Educational Psychology, 85*, 571–581.

7. National Research Council and Institute of Medicine. (2004). *Engaging schools: Fostering high school students' motivation to learn.* Washington, DC: National Academy Press.

8. McLaughlin, M., Irby, M., & Langman, J. (1994). *Urban sanctuaries: Neighborhood organizations in the lives and futures of inner-city youth.* San Francisco: Jossey-Bass.

9. Bartko, W. T., & Eccles, J. (2003). Adolescent participation in structured and unstructured activities: A person-oriented analysis. *Journal of Youth and Adolescence, 32*(4), 233–241.

W. TODD BARTKO *was the executive director of the MacArthur Foundation's Research Network on Successful Pathways Through Middle Childhood and is now an independent consultant in Ann Arbor, Michigan.*

Experience sampling methodology was used to measure engagement during the after-school hours. Experiences that combined high levels of intrinsic motivation with concerted effort and enjoyment were more likely at after-school programs than elsewhere.

7

Activities, engagement, and emotion in after-school programs (and elsewhere)

*Deborah Lowe Vandell, David J. Shernoff,
Kim M. Pierce, Daniel M. Bolt,
Kimberly Dadisman, B. Bradford Brown*

EXPERIENCES THAT ARE deeply engaging and enjoyable, engender full concentration, and present a balance between challenge and skill propel or push development forward.[1] For the past twenty years, researchers have sought to locate environments in which this combination of effort, skill, interest, and enjoyment is more likely. In one study of white middle-class youth, for example, Larson compared adolescents' experiences at school, at home, and during structured voluntary activities (organized sports and community service, for example) and found that these settings differed markedly.[2] During classwork and homework, adolescents reported high levels of concentration and challenge but low levels of intrinsic motivation. While watching television and while hanging out with friends, students reported low concentration and effort but high intrinsic

NEW DIRECTIONS FOR YOUTH DEVELOPMENT, NO. 105, SPRING 2005 © WILEY PERIODICALS, INC.

motivation. It was primarily during voluntary structured activities that youth reported experiencing high levels of intrinsic motivation *and* effort *and* concentration—the combination of engaging experience that propels development forward.

We have extended Larson's work by conducting a research study focusing on the experiences of ethnically and economically diverse youth who attended after-school programs. These youth resided in three states and attended eight different middle schools. Some of the youth, whom we called *program youth*, participated in school-based after-school programs during at least part of the after-school hours. Others, whom we called *nonprogram youth*, did not.

We were interested in two questions. The first pertained to the experiences of the program youth. We asked, "Do youth who attend after-school programs engage in different activities and experience different motivational and emotional states when they are at the after-school programs than when they are elsewhere?" "Elsewhere" was typically their own home, but could also be someone else's home, an outdoor space, or public buildings. The second question then pertained to the after-school time that program and nonprogram youth spend elsewhere. Here we asked, "Are there differences in how program and nonprogram youth spend their time when the program youth are not at the program?"

This second question is important for several reasons. If program and nonprogram students differ in their activities, emotions, and motivation when they are elsewhere, that finding could suggest that program youth differ a priori in fundamental ways from youth who do not attend programs. These preexisting differences in motivation, affect, and engagement could then account for ostensible program effects. Another possibility, however, is that participation in after-school programs has an impact on how youth spend their time even when they are not at the program. In that case, we would expect to see program youth become more productively engaged over the school year, even when they are elsewhere. A third possibility is that program and nonprogram youth do not differ in their experiences when they are elsewhere. In this third case, we would have evidence that differences observed at the program are more likely explained by the program context, not by child differences. We considered each of these possibilities.

A methodology for measuring engagement

Studying activities, emotions, and engagement during the after-school hours is challenging. Activities occur in multiple locations, and it is difficult for observers to follow youth for extended periods as they move from home to school to programs. Teenagers also spend considerable time alone and with unsupervised peers during the nonschool hours, situations that are fundamentally altered when an observer is present. Observers also have difficulty reliably seeing adolescents' feeling states and motivation because youth are adept at masking these feelings.

To address these challenges, we used experience sampling methodology.[3] In this methodology, youth are equipped with logbooks and watches that are programmed to signal at random times. When signaled, youth record their location, social partners, activity, and feelings. The methodology is portable and adaptable; youth can be alone or with others at any location, including home, school, shopping malls or other public places, and after-school programs. They provide self-reports of their feeling states and experiences.

In the study examined here, 191 middle school youth (52 percent male, 60 percent children of color, 47 percent poor or near-poor) wore watches that were programmed to beep thirty-five times during one week in the fall and thirty-five times during one week in the spring of the school year. Signals occurred at random times during the after-school hours, evenings, and weekends. At each signal, the youth recorded who was with them, where they were, and what they were doing. Using a four-point scale, they also rated their responses to seven questions:

1. How much choice do you have about this activity?
2. How important is this activity to you?
3. Is it interesting?

4. Do you enjoy what you are doing?

5. How hard are you concentrating?

6. Are you using your skills?

7. Do you wish you were doing something else?

Their answers reflected three factors: concerted effort (challenge, skills, and concentration), intrinsic motivation (enjoyment, choice, and interest), and importance (a stand-alone item). Youth also reported, using a four-point scale, their feeling states with respect to eleven emotions (happy, proud, excited, relaxed, sad, angry, worried, scared, stressed, bored, and lonely), which were consistent with three factors that we labeled positive emotions, negative emotions, and apathy.

Findings

The youth responded, on average, to thirty-three of the thirty-five signals in the fall and thirty-three of the thirty-five signals in the spring, for a total of 12,143 reports. Of these experiences, 4,846 occurred after school between school dismissal and 6:00 P.M. During these after-school hours, program youth (n = 160) reported participating in an after-school program for at least one signal. They responded to 4,089 signals during weekday afternoons between school dismissal and 6:00 P.M.; 1,030 of these signals occurred when they were at a program, and 3,059 occurred when they were not at a program. Nonprogram youth (n = 31) responded to 759 signals during the weekday afternoons. All of these signals by definition occurred when students were not at a program or structured activity.

The upper half of Table 7.1 shows the proportions of time that program youth spent in different types of activities while at the after-school program and the proportions of time in these activities when the program youth were elsewhere during the after-school hours. Asterisks in column 5 indicate when these proportions were significantly different. As shown in the table, we found pervasive differences. In particular, program youth spent higher proportions of time in academic and arts enrichment, organized sports and physi-

Table 7.1. Comparison of activities and feeling states at after-school programs and elsewhere during the after-school hours

	Program youth at program: (1) % of 1,030 signals	Program youth "elsewhere": (2) % of 3,059 signals	Nonprogram youth ("elsewhere"): (3) % of 759 signals	1 versus 2[a]	2 versus 3[b]
Activity					
Academic/arts enrichment	22.4	7.6	7.7	***	
Sports	26.9	7.6	8.9	***	
Community service	2.6	0.0	0.2	***	
Homework	15.2	9.4	10.2	***	
Snacks/meals	5.5	7.9	10.1	**	*
TV	5.0	18.5	19.0	***	
Socializing with peers	8.1	11.0	8.2	*	*
Feeling states		*Mean Ratings*			
Intrinsic motivation	3.0	2.8	2.8	***	
Concerted effort	2.6	1.8	2.0	***	
Importance	3.0	2.5	2.6	***	
Positive emotion	2.5	2.3	2.3	**	
Negative emotion	1.3	1.3	1.3		
Apathy	1.4	1.5	1.5	***	

[a]Significance levels marked in this column refer to the difference between program youth at the program versus program youth elsewhere (a within-subject comparison), using a two-level hierarchical generalized linear model (HGLM). *p < .05. **p < .01. ***p < .001.

[b]Significance levels marked in this column refer to a difference between program and nonprogram youth when they were elsewhere (a between-subject comparison), as tested by a two-level HGLM model. *p < .05.

cal activities, community service, and homework while they were at the program than elsewhere. They spent less time eating and watching TV while at the program than elsewhere. These differences in activities have important implications for youth development because there is evidence that adolescents who participate in structured activities such as community service and organized sports engage in less antisocial behavior like shoplifting, getting drunk, destroying things, fighting, and skipping school;[4] are less likely to drop out of school or be arrested;[5] and obtain higher ratings of positive social behaviors from teachers and higher achievement test scores.[6] Watching TV and eating, in contrast, are implicated in increased risks for obesity and weight-related health problems.[7]

Table 7.1 also shows that when not at the program during the after-school hours, program youth engaged in activities at similar rates as nonprogram youth. Significant differences emerged for only two activities (see column 6). In comparison to nonprogram youth, program youth spent less time snacking/eating and more time socializing with peers when they were elsewhere. In analyses not shown in the table, we did not find changes from fall to spring in adolescents' activities when they were elsewhere, suggesting that these differences may be child (not program) effects.

The lower half of Table 7.1 reports the adolescents' ratings of engagement and emotion during the after-school hours. Once again, asterisks in column 5 designate significant differences in program youths' experiences at the program and elsewhere. Program youth reported feeling more intrinsically motivated and putting forth more concerted effort, and experienced their activities as more important, at programs versus elsewhere. Program youth also reported feeling less apathy and more positive emotions at after-school programs than elsewhere. When elsewhere, however, program and nonprogram youth did not differ significantly in their feelings of intrinsic motivation, concerted effort, or positive emotions (see column 6).

Finally, we considered the likelihood of youth experiencing four combinations of feeling states during the after-school hours. The first combination consisted of high choice in conjunction with high concentration. Larson posited that this combination of motivational states is important for the development of initiative because it combines intrinsic motivation with concerted effort.[8] The second combination was a high degree of choice of the activity but low concentration, a combination consistent with leisure and relaxation. The third combination consisted of low choice and high concentration, a combination of feeling states that is often reported during the school day. The final combination consisted of low choice and low concentration, which occurs when individuals are disengaged.

As shown in Table 7.2, program youth were almost twice as likely to experience high choice in combination with high concentration while they were at the after-school program (40 percent of the time) than elsewhere (21 percent). They also were more likely to experience low choice and high concentration at programs versus elsewhere, which occurred primarily when they were getting homework help. When the program youth were elsewhere, the high choice and low concentration combination (consistent with leisure and relaxation) was more likely (52 percent of the time versus 34 percent of the adolescents' time at programs).

Nonprogram youth did not differ in their combined feelings of choice and concentration from program youth when elsewhere. Low choice in combination with low concentration, a feeling state consistent with disengagement, was reported at almost one-quarter of the signals when the youth were not at the after-school programs.

Table 7.2. Proportion of time spent in different choice and concentration combinations

	Program youth at program: (1) % of 1,030 signals	Program youth "elsewhere": (2) % of 3,059 signals	Nonprogram youth ("elsewhere"): (3) % of 759 signals	1 versus 2[a]	2 versus 3[b]
High choice and high concentration	39.7	21.1	25.3	***	
High choice and low concentration	33.8	52.2	46.5	***	
Low choice and high concentration	14.9	9.5	10.1	***	
Low choice and low concentration	15.7	22.4	22.4	***	

[a]Significance levels marked in this column refer to the difference between program youth at the program versus program youth elsewhere (a within-subject comparison), using a two-level hierarchical generalized linear model (HGLM). ***$p < .001$.

[b]The absence of asterisks in this column indicates that significant differences were not detected between program and nonprogram youth when they were elsewhere, as tested by a two-level HGLM model.

Conclusion

From these analyses, we conclude that school-based after-school programs provide youth with substantially different opportunities and experiences than they would otherwise have. Youth spend more time doing sports, art and academic enrichment, community service, and homework at programs versus elsewhere. They devote less of their after-school hours to watching TV and eating. While engaging in these activities at programs, they experience more intrinsic motivation, put forth more concerted effort, and feel less apathetic, underscoring the potential of after-school programs as a positive developmental context. The potential import of after-school programs was underscored by our analyses of the time that youth spent elsewhere. For the most part, the after-school hours of the program and nonprogram youth did not differ when they were elsewhere. Both program and nonprogram youth spent their unstructured time watching TV, eating, and socializing with peers. In these unstructured settings, the youth reported feelings of apathy and disengagement. The similarities in these experiences while elsewhere point to the program context rather than child differences as the reason that high-quality after-school programs are linked to positive youth development. Finally, these findings support the utility of expanding the conceptualization of program participation to consider time in specific activities and the feeling states that accompany those activities. As these findings demonstrate, it is possible to reliably assess engagement by asking adolescents about their feelings and experiences. In our study, we used experience sampling to measure motivation, effort, and emotion. In other projects, however, we have questionnaires or surveys to assess engagement more globally. Both approaches provide windows onto student engagement that can be used in program evaluations.

Notes

1. Csikszentmihalyi, M. (1990). *Flow*. New York: HarperCollins.

2. Larson, R. W. (1994). Youth organizations, hobbies, and sports as developmental contexts. In R. K. Silbereisen & E. Todt (Eds.), *Adolescence in con-*

text: The interplay of family, school, peers, and work in adjustment (pp. 46–65). New York: Springer-Verlag.

3. Csikszentmihalyi, M., & Larson, R. (1987). Validity and reliability of experience sampling method. *Journal of Nervous and Mental Disease, 175*(9), 526–536.

4. Mahoney, J. L. (2000). School extracurricular activity participation as a moderator in the development of antisocial patterns. *Child Development, 71,* 502–516.

5. Mahoney, J. L., & Stattin, H. (2000). Leisure activities and adolescent antisocial behavior: The role of structure and social context. *Journal of Adolescence, 23,* 113–127.

6. Casey, D. M., Ripke, M. N., & Huston, A. C. (in press). Activity participation and the well-being of children and adolescents in the context of welfare reform. In J. L. Mahoney, R. W. Larson, & J. S. Eccles (Eds.), *Organized activities as contexts of development: Extracurricular activities, after school and community programs.* Mahwah, NJ: Erlbaum.

7. American Academy of Pediatrics. (2003). Prevention of pediatric overweight and obesity. *Pediatrics, 112*(2), 424–430.

8. Larson, R. W. (2000). Toward a psychology of positive youth development. *American Psychologist, 55*(1), 170–183.

DEBORAH LOWE VANDELL *is the Sears Bascom Professor in Education at the University of Wisconsin, Madison.*

DAVID J. SHERNOFF *is an assistant professor in the Department of Leadership, Educational Psychology and Foundations at Northern Illinois University.*

KIM M. PIERCE *is a research scientist at the Wisconsin Center of Education Research at the University of Wisconsin, Madison.*

DANIEL M. BOLT *is an associate professor in the Department of Educational Psychology at the University of Wisconsin, Madison.*

KIMBERLY DADISMAN *is a researcher at the Wisconsin Center for Education Research at the University of Wisconsin, Madison.*

B. BRADFORD BROWN *is a professor of educational psychology at the University of Wisconsin, Madison.*

Index

KidTrax, 95

Laird, R. D., 97
Larson, R. W., 19, 121, 122, 126
Latino youth, 35, 36–45
Lauver, S. C., 7, 11–12, 71
Leadership skills, 26, 83–85, 84
Learn and Serve America, 84
Learning: in effective programs, 46t;
   and engagement, 113, 114; as participation reason, 38
Little, P.M.D., 2, 6, 7, 8, 9–10, 11–12,
   15, 19, 71, 95, 96, 97, 99, 111
Low-income children: challenges of
   serving, 34, 53; participation discrepancies involving, 15–16; participation patterns of, 52–53;
   problems of, 54; and project-
   oriented activities, 82; types of
   activities of, 65. See also Minority
   children

Management, 92
Marshall, N., 54
Maryland After School Community
   Grant Program, 18
McCurdy, K., 22
McLaughlin, M., 2, 118
Middle school, 18
Middle-income children, 53, 54, 65
Minority children: participation dis-
   crepancies involving, 15–16; partic-
   ipation study of, 36–45; rationale
   for studying participation of,
   34–35. See also Low-income
   children
Motivation, 19, 125t; during academic
   work, 121, 122; versus engagement,
   24; and environment, 116

Needs assessment, 74
Neighborhoods, 22, 53
Nellie Mae Education Foundation, 6
New Hope study, 52, 57–67
Noam, G. G., 4

Obesity, 126
Orientation, 80
Out-of-School Time Evaluation Data-
   base, 7, 72

Out-of-school-time programs: benefits
   of, 15, 16, 17, 44; definition of, 6,
   27n.1; past research in, 109–110;
   recent interest in, 109. See also
   After-school programs

P. F. Bresee Foundation, 93
Participant outcomes, 94
Participation: and academic beliefs, 64;
   and academic success, 63–64; barriers to, 18–19; and behavior, 64;
   benefits of, 44, 51–52; Childhood
   and Beyond study of, 52, 55–57,
   59–67; conceptual model of, 20–25;
   definition of, 19; demonstrating
   importance of, 76; and developmental outcomes, 54–55, 66; discrepancies in, 15–16; expectation
   for, 25–26; incentives for, 82–83; of
   low-income children, 52–53; measurement of, 26–27; New Hope
   study of, 52, 57–67; overview of,
   33–34; predictors of, 21f, 22, 27;
   rationale for studying minority
   youth's, 34–35; recommendations
   to increase, 45–47; recruitment
   strategies to enhance, 79–85; selection bias in, 34; systemic view of,
   27; youth's reasons against, 35–36,
   39–41; youth's reasons for, 35,
   38–39
Participation equation: definition of, 6;
   implications of, 20; overview of, 16,
   19–20; in participation model, 21f,
   22; research and participation
   issues involving, 25–27
Passmore, A., 35
Peer pressure, 40
Perkins, D. F., 6–7, 10, 33
Petit, G. S., 97
Pierce, K. M., 7, 13–14, 121
Planning, 92
Policymakers: questions of, 16
Program leaders, 117
Program quality: attendance measure-
   ment to monitor, 94; critical ele-
   ments of, 72–74; importance of, 25;
   and reasons against participation,
   40
Program youth, 122
Project-oriented activities, 82

Notes for Contributors

New Directions for Youth Development: Theory, Practice, and Research is a quarterly publication focusing on current contemporary issues challenging the field of youth development. A defining focus of the journal is the relationship among theory, research, and practice. In particular, *NDYD* is dedicated to recognizing resilience as well as risk, and healthy development of our youth as well as the difficulties of adolescence. The journal is intended as a forum for provocative discussion that reaches across the worlds of academia, service, philanthropy, and policy.

In the tradition of the New Directions series, each volume of the journal addresses a single, timely topic, although special issues covering a variety of topics are occasionally commissioned. We welcome submissions of both volume topics and individual articles. All articles should specifically address the implications of theory for practice and research directions, and how these arenas can better inform one another. Articles may focus on any aspect of youth development; all theoretical and methodological orientations are welcome.

If you would like to be an *issue editor,* please submit an outline of no more than four pages (single spaced, 12 point type) that includes a brief description of your proposed topic and its significance along with a brief synopsis of individual articles (including tentative authors and a working title for each chapter).

If you would like to be an *author,* please submit first a draft of an abstract of no more than 1,500 words, including a two-sentence synopsis of the article; send this to the managing editor.

For all prospective issue editors or authors:

- Please make sure to keep accessibility in mind, by illustrating theoretical ideas with specific examples and explaining technical terms in nontechnical language. A busy practitioner who may not have an extensive research background should be well served by our work.

- Please keep in mind that references should be limited to twenty-five to thirty. Authors should make use of case examples to illustrate their ideas, rather than citing exhaustive research references. You may want to recommend two or three key articles, books, or Websites that are influential in the field, to be featured on a resource page. This can be used by readers who want to delve more deeply into a particular topic.
- All reference information should be listed as endnotes, rather than including author names in the body of the article or footnotes at the bottom of the page.

Please visit http://ndyd.org for more information.

Back Issue/Subscription Order Form

Copy or detach and send to:

Jossey-Bass, A Wiley Company, 989 Market Street, San Francisco, CA 94103-1741

Call or fax toll-free: Phone 888-378-2537 6:30AM – 3PM PST; Fax 888-481-2665

Back Issues: Please send me the following issues at $29 each
(Important: please include series initials and issue number, such as YD100.)

_____

_____

_____

$ _____   Total for single issues

$ _____   SHIPPING CHARGES: SURFACE   Domestic   Canadian
                                      First Item $5.00 $6.00
                                      Each Add'l Item $3.00 $1.50
                    For next-day and second-day delivery rates, call the number listed above.

Subscriptions: Please __start __renew my subscription to *New Directions for Youth Development* for the year 2_____ at the following rate:

U.S.	__Individual $80	__Institutional $170
Canada	__Individual $80	__Institutional $210
All Others	__Individual $104	__Institutional $244

**For more information about online subscriptions visit
www.interscience.wiley.com**

$ _____   Total single issues and subscriptions (Add appropriate sales tax for your state for single issue orders. No sales tax for U.S. subscriptions. Canadian residents, add GST for subscriptions and single issues.)

__Payment enclosed (U.S. check or money order only)
__VISA __MC __AmEx #_____ Exp. Date _____

Signature _____ Day Phone _____
__ Bill Me (U.S. institutional orders only. Purchase order required.)

Purchase order # _____
                Federal Tax ID13559302   **GST 89102 8052**

Name _____

Address _____

_____

Phone _____ E-mail _____

For more information about Jossey-Bass, visit our Web site at **www.josseybass.com**

NEW DIRECTIONS FOR YOUTH DEVELOPMENT
IS NOW AVAILABLE ONLINE AT WILEY INTERSCIENCE

What is Wiley InterScience?

Wiley InterScience is the dynamic online content service from John Wiley & Sons delivering the full text of over 300 leading scientific, technical, medical, and professional journals, plus major reference works, the acclaimed *Current Protocols* laboratory manuals, and even the full text of select Wiley print books online.

What are some special features of Wiley InterScience?

Wiley InterScience Alerts is a service that delivers table of contents via e-mail for any journal available on Wiley InterScience as soon as a new issue is published online.
Early View is Wiley's exclusive service presenting individual articles online as soon as they are ready, even before the release of the compiled print issue. These articles are complete, peer-reviewed, and citable.
CrossRef is the innovative multi-publisher reference linking system enabling readers to move seamlessly from a reference in a journal article to the cited publication, typically located on a different server and published by a different publisher.

How can I access Wiley InterScience?

Visit http://www.interscience.wiley.com

Guest Users can browse Wiley InterScience for unrestricted access to journal Tables of Contents and Article Abstracts, or use the powerful search engine.
Registered Users are provided with a *Personal Home Page* to store and manage customized alerts, searches, and links to favorite journals and articles. Additionally, Registered Users can view free Online Sample Issues and preview selected material from major reference works.
Licensed Customers are entitled to access full-text journal articles in PDF, with select journals also offering full-text HTML.

How do I become an Authorized User?

Authorized Users are individuals authorized by a paying Customer to have access to the journals in Wiley InterScience. For example, a university that subscribes to Wiley journals is considered to be the Customer. Faculty, staff and students authorized by the university to have access to those journals in Wiley InterScience are Authorized Users. Users should contact their Library for information on which Wiley journals they have access to in Wiley InterScience.

ASK YOUR INSTITUTION ABOUT WILEY INTERSCIENCE TODAY!